MOUNTAIN WALKING IN SNOWDONIA

40 OF THE FINEST ROUTES IN SNOWDONIA

About the Author

Terry Fletcher has been walking and climbing in Snowdonia for almost 50 years since first visiting the Llanberis Pass as an awestruck teenage rock climber. Since then these romantic mountains have drawn him back again and again to climb on some of the most famous rock faces in Britain and to scramble on the high ridges. Although a proud Yorkshireman (is there any other kind?) he also claims Welsh blood on his mother's side. He has walked, skied and climbed extensively throughout Europe and North America and has a particular love for the sandstone deserts and canyons of the American South West. He has been a full-time professional writer for more than 40 years, writing for almost every national newspaper as well as specialist magazines and appearing on television and radio to comment on the outdoors. He is a former editor of *Countryman*, *Dalesman* and *Cumbria* magazines and was a senior executive at the *Yorkshire Post*. He still lives in the Yorkshire Dales.

Other Cicerone guides by the author
Walking on the Costa Blanca

MOUNTAIN WALKING IN SNOWDONIA

40 OF THE FINEST ROUTES IN SNOWDONIA

by Terry Fletcher

JUNIPER HOUSE, MURLEY MOSS,
OXENHOLME ROAD, KENDAL, CUMBRIA LA9 7RL
www.cicerone.co.uk

© Terry Fletcher 2016
First edition 2016
ISBN: 978 1 85284 767 8
Reprinted 2018 (with updates)

Printed in China on behalf of Latitude Press Ltd
A catalogue record for this book is available from the British Library.
All photographs are by the author unless otherwise stated.

© Crown copyright 2016 OS PU100012932

Map data

Updates to this Guide

While every effort is made by our authors to ensure the accuracy of guidebooks as they go to print, changes can occur during the lifetime of an edition. Any updates that we know of for this guide will be on the Cicerone website (www.cicerone. co.uk/767updates), so please check before planning your trip. We also advise that you check information about such things as transport, accommodation and shops locally. Even rights of way can be altered over time. We are always grateful for information about any discrepancies between a guidebook and the facts on the ground, sent by email to updates@cicerone.co.uk or by post to Cicerone, Juniper House, Murley Moss, Oxenholme Road, Kendal LA9 7RL.

Register your book: To sign up to receive free updates, special offers and GPX files where available, register your book at www.cicerone.co.uk.

Mountain safety

Every mountain walk has its dangers, and those described in this guidebook are no exception. All who walk or climb in the mountains should recognise this and take responsibility for themselves and their companions along the way. The author and publisher have made every effort to ensure that the information contained in this guide was correct when it went to press, but, except for any liability that cannot be excluded by law, they cannot accept responsibility for any loss, injury or inconvenience sustained by any person using this book.

To call out the Mountain Rescue, ring 999 (in the UK) or the international emergency number 112: this will connect you via any available network. Once connected to the emergency operator, ask for the police.

Front cover: Crib Goch

CONTENTS

Route symbols on OS map extracts
(for OS legend see printed OS maps)

Features on the overview map

 route

link route A

 National Park
eg **SNOWDONIA**

 start/finish point

 start point

 finish point

 alternative start/finish point

Area of Outstanding Natural
Beauty/National Scenic Area
eg *Anglesey*

800m
600m
400m
200m
75m
0m

 route direction

All maps are 1:50,000 except Routes 8, 9, 10, 11,13, 20 and 30 which are 1:25,000

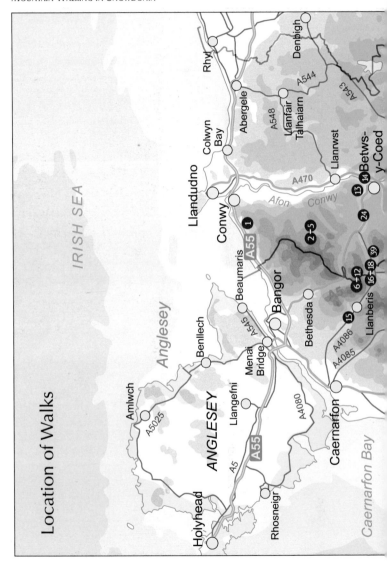

Location of Walks

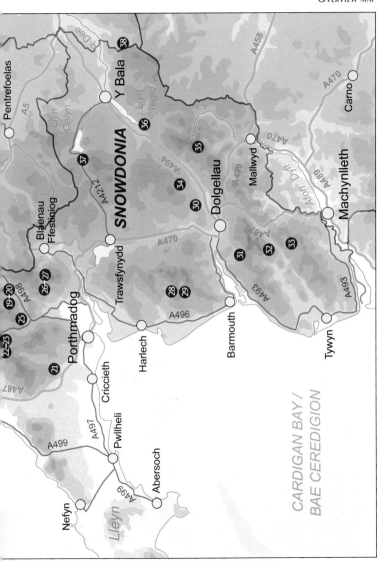

Walkers descending Watkin Path from Snowdon

INTRODUCTION

Lliwedd, the last nail in the Snowdon Horseshoe (Walk 16)

Snowdonia can justifiably lay claim to the finest mountain walking in Britain. That's a bold statement to make but the only serious challengers are the Scottish Highlands and the English Lake District and this magical, mystical corner of Wales contrives to combine the best features of both.

The mountains in the north of Snowdonia National Park are big and raw-boned, matching the majesty of their Scottish counterparts. Rock is never far from the surface, giving them a challengingly rugged texture. They are armour-plated with vast sweeps of naked stone and embossed with crags that gleam in the sunshine and glower in the rain. They are indelibly scarred by deep, rocky cwms where long-gone glaciers have taken huge bites

from their flanks. They bristle with jagged ridges, which set scramblers' pulses racing and spirits soaring, and are crowned by sharp, spiky summits.

At the same time, like the Lakeland Fells they are closely packed, clustered round intimate valleys and bound together by high ridges that lend themselves to satisfying horseshoes or long, high-level treks, picking off summits as you go.

They are also in exactly the right place, sufficiently close to the major centres of population to be accessible for a fleeting weekend yet just far enough away to retain an essential aura of remoteness. The widespread use of Welsh as the day-to-day language of the locals, overheard in villages with near-unpronounceable, tongue-twisting names, only adds to their sense of otherworldliness.

They also have an extra dimension that only proximity to two coasts can bring. With the Menai Straits to the north and the great sweep of Cardigan Bay to the west, the sea is a feature in many a summit view, projecting its own constantly changing charm and ever-shifting light. There are few pleasures to match dropping into a swiftly darkening valley after witnessing the sun sink into a blood-red sea.

And they pack in an astonishing variety. At first glance the Carneddau in the north seem to be huge, grassy mounds, but closer exploration reveals that they are not without drama, as some of the national park's most impressive and least frequented crags are tucked away beneath their seemingly innocuous flanks. Across the

deep trench of the Nant Ffrancon stand the Glyderau, huge, crag-girt fortresses of solid stone which rival and sometimes even outshine Snowdon itself in their rocky challenges, especially on the sharp crest of Tryfan.

But Snowdon will not be outdone. Although surrounded by a cluster of equally dramatic acolytes, the highest mountain south of the Roman Wall refuses to be ignored and seldom is. Don't expect to have it to yourself, no matter how unpromising the weather may be. The Horseshoe, starting on the tightrope of Crib Goch and ending on the double summit of Y Lliwedd, is unrivalled as the area's most famous and most challenging short(ish) walk, a must for every ambitious walker and scrambler. In all, 15 peaks that top the magic 3000ft contour are crammed into this northern sector of the park.

Sychnant Pass in the Carneddau (Walk 1)

Tryfan's North Ridge (Walk 8)

The Welsh 3000s

Snowdon	
Snowdon/Yr Wyddfa	3560ft (1085m)
Garnedd Ugain/Crib y Ddysgl	3494ft (1065m)
Crib Goch	3028ft (923m)
Glyderau	
Elidir Fawr	3031ft (924m)
Y Garn	3107ft (947m)
Glyder Fawr	3283ft (999m)
Glyder Fach	3262ft (994m)

Tryfan	3002ft (915m)
Carneddau	
Pen yr Ole Wen	3208ft (978m)
Carnedd Dafydd	3425ft (1044m)
Carnedd Llewelyn	3490ft (1064m)
Yr Elen	3156ft (962m)
Foel Grach	3201ft (976m)
Garnedd Uchaf/Gwenllian	3038ft (926m)
Foel-fras	3089ft (942m)

To the south the heights diminish – although Cadair Idris, a scant 71ft shy of the magic figure, can hold its own in any company – and the valleys soften a little but the mountains lose nothing of their challenge and character. Each range – the Moelwyns, Rhinogs, Arans, Arenigs and Tarrens – has its own appeal and character. They are by turns magnificent, magical and melancholy. These are big mountains with big personalities and they leave an indelible impression.

The Miners' Track with (l to r) Lliwedd, Snowdon and Crib Goch beyond (Walk 17)

There is a Welsh word, *hiraeth*, which defies exact translation into English but might best be rendered as 'a wistful longing for Wales'. Spend much time among these mountains and anyone with an ounce of romance in their soul will learn its meaning, and will feel the deep pull of these mountains whenever they are far away.

GEOLOGY

Although relatively compact, at just 2132km² (823 square miles) Snowdonia reveals an astonishingly diverse geology born of fire, water and ice. The most eye-catching peaks, such as Snowdon itself, the Glyderau and Carneddau are the children of long-extinct volcanoes that spewed out molten lava to create rock

hard-wearing enough to resist the glaciers of the last Ice Age, which gouged huge valleys and hanging cwms from the mountainsides more than 10,000 years ago.

Yet almost as significant – perhaps even more so in the life and history of the area – are the sedimentary rocks, laid down on ocean floors and long-vanished estuaries. Today the most noticeable of these are the huge slate deposits which, in turn, spawned the vast caverns, quarries and spoil heaps that still overshadow the towns of Llanberis and Blaenau Ffestiniog. But scarcely a hillside or a valley totally escaped the delvers and quarrymen, and almost every view will include at least some workings, no matter how small.

To the west the Rhinogs, overlooking the sea, contain another

Cwm Idwal (Walk 10)

geological surprise with outcrops of gritstone, more usually associated with the Pennines and the Peak District. This is a land of constant revelations, where nothing can be taken for granted.

HISTORY

The story of man is written deep into this landscape although, this being Wales, it can sometimes be hard to differentiate myth and legend from fact. Early man certainly left his mark in the shape of stone circles and standing stones, such as those seen on Tal y Fan (Walk 1), as well as in huge mounds of stones, built for unknown purposes with enormous effort on some of the highest peaks.

Later men built even bigger mounds of stones in the quest for slate. This was already an industry when the Romans arrived in the area, and the earliest written records date from the 14th century. Large-scale production began towards the end of the 18th century, with the need to roof the booming towns and cities of the Industrial Revolution, and by Victorian times Wales was the biggest slate producer in the world, with much of its output coming from the north.

Between pre-history and modern times came the rise and fall of the independent Princes of Wales, who finally perished in bitter wars with the English. The names of the last two are commemorated in the names of great peaks, Carnedd Llywelyn and Carnedd Dafydd, but works of the English victors are more ubiquitous, in the form of a ring of grim fortresses,

15

Harlech Castle

such as Conwy, Caernarfon and Harlech, built to subdue the locals.

WILDLIFE

With its wide range of habitats, from high mountains to lush valleys, Snowdonia is home to an astonishing array of species, including some, like the Snowdon lily – the emblem of the national park – which are unique to the area. Another rarity is the Gwyniad, a unique sub-species of fish which lives in Llyn Tegid (Bala Lake), where it was trapped after the last Ice Age 10,000 years ago.

Otters and polecats are to be seen in the park, and the shy pine marten is thought to breed in the extensive conifer forests, although it is hard to track down. In the air birds of prey, notably peregrine falcon, merlin and

The Snowdon Lily is the emblem of the national park

Ravens are frequently seen on the highest ground

use public transport the area has two main network railway lines. The holiday resorts of the north are served by the North Wales Coast Line, which runs on to Bangor and Holyhead and also has connections down the Conwy Valley Line to Betws-y-Coed and Blaenau Ffestiniog. The Cambrian line comes in from the south east via Shrewsbury and Welshpool and then up the coast to Porthmadog and Pwllheli. National Express Coaches also serve the area.

GETTING AROUND

It must be admitted that a car is the most convenient form of transport for walkers, especially for reaching some of the more out-of-the-way starting points: however, Snowdonia does enjoy some wonderful alternative transport options. Perhaps the most romantic are the 'Great Little Trains' – the preserved and restored lines that once served the thriving slate mines but which now carry tourists, bustling and wheezing their way through the very heart of the mountains. The combined Ffestiniog and Welsh Highland Railway offers a wonderful way to reach some of the routes, notably Walks 22 and 23 which start at Rhyd-Ddu station and Walk 25 starting from Beddgelert. The 200-year-old Ffestiniog Railway, running 22km (13½ miles) from the harbour at Porthmadog to Blaenau, claims to be the oldest narrow gauge railway in the world and runs three

red kite, patrol the skies. Ravens are frequent visitors to the highest ground although, given the proximity of the coast, you are just as likely to share the summits with gulls, which have learned that there are easy pickings to be had from walkers' rucksacks. Osprey also breed at Glaslyn, near Porthmadog, where a viewing station has been set up.

Some of the easiest 'wildlife' to spot are the semi-wild ponies which graze the Carneddau, and the feral goats which are to be found almost everywhere.

GETTING THERE

Most visitors will arrive by car from the M6 motorway, either via the A5 or along the much-improved A55 coast road. For those who prefer to engines which are over 150 years old yet still manage to climb 215m (700ft) into the mountains. The Welsh Highland's claim is to be longest heritage railway in the UK, running 40km (25 miles) from Caernarfon to Porthmadog via Beddgelert. In the south, squeezing between Cadair Idris and the Tarrens, the Talyllyn (this time the oldest preserved railway) runs 12km (7½ miles) from Tywyn to Nant Gwernol, and serves Walk 33. There is also, of course, the railway up Snowdon, but that's hardly relevant to this guidebook other than as either a quirky novelty or intrusive irritant, depending on your point of view.

Less romantic but perhaps more useful are the local buses, particularly the Snowdon Sherpa which has routes to Betws-y-Coed and Capel Curig as well as the Ogwen and Llanberis passes.

Details of services change to a greater or lesser degree each season but Conwy Council (www.conwy. gov.uk) has published a combined timetable which draws together local bus services. This is also available from tourist offices and is very useful for planning journeys which may entail routes operated by different companies.

WHERE TO STAY

Snowdonia is a big place – more than 80km (50 miles) from north to south – and mountain roads are not the fastest, especially at peak holiday periods. So it pays to pick a base which will allow you to explore a given area, rather than trying to cover the whole

Beddgelert is well placed for walking

Tal-y-Lyn

park in a single trip. Fortunately most places are supplied with a variety of accommodation, from basic campsites and bunkhouses, to youth hostels, B&Bs, pubs and hotels.

For the Ogwen Valley, Bethesda and Capel Curig offer plenty of options with a youth hostel and camping at Ogwen itself. Betws-y-Coed is also an attractive option with plenty of hotels, B&Bs and campsites for those who prefer a greater choice and a more picturesque setting. For Snowdon and the Glyders the youth hostel at Pen-y-Pass could not be better placed, on a high col between the two ranges, though some may find it a little isolated on its high perch. Llanberis at the foot of the eponymous pass is a popular though less picturesque option.

Beddgelert is another attractive village, well placed for walking and with plenty of accommodation options. Visitors to the southern part of the national park may want to consider Bala or Dolgellau, while out west the coastal towns and villages around Harlech and Abermaw/Barmouth and the idyllic Mawddach Estuary have bags of appeal, especially if a walking trip is being combined with a family beach holiday.

WHEN TO GO

There's no getting away from the fact that Snowdonia can be a bit moist. In fact it is officially one of the wettest places in the UK, which will come a no surprise to regular visitors, boasting – if that's the right word – more

19

Llyn y Cwn and Tryfan (Walk 12)

than 4.4m (15ft) of rainfall in some years on Crib Goch. That's a lot of rain in anyone's book, but there are plenty of fine days too.

Like all mountains, Snowdonia's tend to make their own weather, and conditions can vary widely across the park. It is possible to stand on one massif in bright sunshine while looking across at Snowdon and the Glyderau swaddled in cloud. The proximity of the sea only complicates matters for the forecasters, but if the cloud on Snowdon is down to your ankles it is sometimes possible to rescue a day by heading south to the lower hills or out to the west to the Lleyn Peninsula, itself an area of outstanding beauty where conditions can be better.

In general, spring and early summer, from April through to June or July, often offer the driest weather.

September and October also give some spectacular days, but August, by contrast, can be disappointing. During the coldest months the closeness of the sea can take the edge off winter temperatures, making them higher than might be expected on such high ground – much to the annoyance of ice climbers. However there are still plenty of days when temperatures at high levels are below freezing, which make conditions treacherous and demand ice axes and crampons. As with many UK mountains their most predictable feature is their sheer unpredictability.

Not surprisingly weekends and school holidays are the busiest times. On the weekends around the longest day in late June people attempting the Three Peaks Challenge – summiting Ben Nevis, Scafell Pike and Snowdon within 24 hours – only add to the crowds, and you may well find yourself queueing along Crib Goch, while the popular PyG Track from the Pen-y-Pass car park to Snowdon's summit can be a crowded trudge.

EQUIPMENT

Clothing will vary with the time of year and from person to person but remember that conditions in the valley may bear little resemblance to those on the tops, where temperatures can be much lower and wind speeds much higher. Make sure your rucksack contains adequate spare clothing and waterproofs, no matter how blue the morning sky may be. Also carry extra food and drink in case of emergencies, or if the day turns out to be longer than expected.

The rucksack should also contain a first aid kit, torch with spare batteries and bulbs if necessary.

Always carry a compass and map. Do not rely solely on the maps in this book, which, to keep things to a manageable size, are mostly based on the Ordnance Survey 1:50,000 scale, although for clarity some of the shorter routes (Routes 8, 9, 10, 11, 13, 20 and 30) are shown at 1:25,000. All show only the immediate area of each walk, so that should you inadvertently walk 'off the edge' you will be lost. Hence it is also recommended that you carry the larger-scale 1:25,000 OS Outdoor Leisure or Explorer maps, as detailed at the beginning of each route, which not only include more detail but will allow you to identify surrounding tops and other features. Harvey Superwalker 1:25,000 maps cover the area, as do the Harvey British Mountain Maps at 1:40,000. Maps should be carried even if you prefer to use a GPS handset to navigate. Paper maps may be scornfully dismissed by some as 'dead tree technology' but at least they never run out of battery at the crucial moment and they still work after being dropped off an outcrop.

MOUNTAIN RESCUE

Snowdonia is covered by several mountain rescue teams, all made up of volunteers who give their valuable time unpaid. Please do not abuse their goodwill by making frivolous calls.

If you do need the team dial 999 and ask for the police, who will alert the appropriate team which will then call you back. Having made the call, keep the line clear. It may seem counter-intuitive, but if you have no signal at the site of an accident it may be easier to find one by gaining rather than losing height, as masts work on line of sight.

To help them get to you quickly make sure you have:
•   the grid reference of the incident
•   the nature of the incident
•   the number of people involved
•   age and medical information on the casualty
•   an alternative phone number if possible.

USING THIS GUIDE

Distances are given in kilometres and miles, heights in metres and feet. Because of the nature of the terrain some of the walks demand a greater degree of mountaincraft than others. Some of the routes, including popular rounds like the Snowdon Horseshoe, ascents of Tryfan and parts of the Glyderau also involve scrambles which call for a certain degree of agility and a head for heights. Please heed the warnings in the text and pick your routes accordingly, using variations where they are given if you are unsure of your ability or if the weather or conditions are against you. Remember the sobering words of the mountaineer Don Whillans, who was no shrinking violet: 'It'll be there next year. The trick is to make sure you are.'

Timings are as walked by me, a bus pass holder with high mileage knees, and are inevitably subjective. They should be treated as a rough guide only until you have walked a few of the routes and had a chance to compare our respective paces and you have got the measure of my timings, which do not allow for stops.

Likewise the grade of difficulty is as I personally found it. Easy routes are fairly gentle strolls. Moderate walks demand more effort and may involve rough going. Strenuous routes are demanding days, often with steep climbs. The scrambles are about Grade 1 but may be exposed. Although they are well used some do call for a little route finding ability.

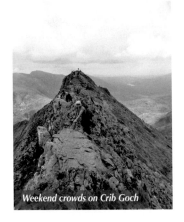
Weekend crowds on Crib Goch

PLACE NAMES

So far as place names are concerned I have tried to use the Welsh wherever practicable while also falling in with general usage. These days most visitors seem happy to use the Carneddau for what used to be called the Carnedds and the Glyderau is also gaining currency over the anglicised Glyders. Snowdon, however, is so far resisting all attempts to re-brand it Yr Wyddfa in the popular consciousness, and the National Park remains resolutely Snowdonia rather than Barc Cenedlaethol Eryri.

Despite my family roots in the Principality I am definitely no Welsh scholar, so where there is a dispute over spelling, such as Cadair/Cader, in the interests of consistency and avoiding confusion with the mapping I have appointed the Ordnance Survey the arbiter of correctness.

THE CARNEDDAU

Pen y Helgi Du (Walk 4)

WALK 1
Tal y Fan

Start/Finish	Sychnant Pass SH 750 769
Distance	16km (10 miles)
Total ascent	510m (1540ft)
Grade	Moderate
Time	4–5hr
Terrain	Moorland tracks
Map	OS OL17 Snowdon/Yr Wyddfa
Access	Via the steep Sychnant Pass road from Conwy to Penmaenmawr
Parking	Roadside at the top of the pass

This is very definitely a walk of two halves. For the first section the Irish Sea and Menai Straits are constant companions, dominating the views as you look down onto the towns of the north coast of Wales. Then as you crest the final ridge of Tal y Fan everything changes as the mountains reassert themselves. Once the path switches to the inland side of the ridge it becomes a hill walk again, as befits Snowdonia's most northerly 2000fter, a distinction it makes by a whisker.

From the top of the pass cross to the western side and go through a gate marked 'Pensychnant Nature Reserve and Farm'. Follow the stony track for a couple of hundred metres and then turn back hard rightwards on a rising path, part of the North Wales Path. After another 50 metres by a waymarker turn left uphill, passing under a set of power lines to climb to another marker post where the path turns right under more power lines before climbing towards the ridge.

Where the track passes under the power lines yet again turn right uphill on a wide track, broadly following the electricity lines across heathery moorland. ◄ At the top of the slope carry on ahead, still following the track

The views stretch to the surrounding headlands and sea and a marine forest of dozens of offshore wind turbines.

parallel to the power lines to reach a stile with white-washed farm buildings below.

The path continues traversing above the farm buildings and then carries on in the same direction briefly following a wall, still guided by the power lines and the occasional waymarker for the North Wales Path.

The path, now much fainter, comes to a group of ruined enclosures containing clumps of trees then continues above them and in a couple of hundred metres comes to a fork. Turn uphill to soon reach a much broader vehicle track coming in from the left. Turn right along this, aiming for the long rocky ridge of **Tal y Fan**.

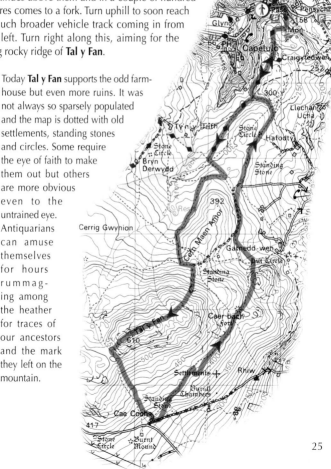

Today **Tal y Fan** supports the odd farmhouse but even more ruins. It was not always so sparsely populated and the map is dotted with old settlements, standing stones and circles. Some require the eye of faith to make them out but others are more obvious even to the untrained eye. Antiquarians can amuse themselves for hours rummaging among the heather for traces of our ancestors and the mark they left on the mountain.

25

A rider heads towards Tal y Fan

The whole atmosphere of the walk now changes as the sea views disappear and the Conwy Valley opens up ahead.

The track passes high above the reed-fringed pool of an old reservoir before it begins to climb slowly leftwards up towards the end of the ridge. At the watershed it meets another vehicle track. Follow this rightwards as it curls round into an area of quarry spoil heaps with fine views of the Conwy Estuary. Once past these a grassy path begins to climb the ridge, weaving its way through rocks and outcrops, guided by a wall, with ever-improving views of the inland hills to arrive at the sturdy stone trig point.

From the summit carry on following the wall to a col and take a stile on the left and go down to another stile in the right hand wall. ◄

The path drops over three stiles to reach a tarmac lane, which is followed leftwards for 50 metres to where an unmade track branches off left. After a couple of hundred metres along this a footpath sign at **Cae Coch** directs you back up the slope. The path follows a gently rising traverse line rightwards across the hillside following the line of a wall. This is a delightful stroll with the ridge above and the woods and fields of the valley of the River

Conwy below. Where the wall becomes dilapidated carry on along the same line as the ridge drops down towards the track.

Eventually after about three quarters of an hour of steady walking the path curls round the hill to slip through a prominent pass and begins to drop down. Where it forks do not follow the main track into the valley but instead follow a wall on the left and look for a gap in the corner ahead about 200m below the col. The track passes through this and then follows the left hand side of the wall along the edge of the moor.

Carry on circling the hill with the intake wall always on your right. The aim is to stay above the intake wall always following the moorland edge.

When the track reaches another pass in the ridge, turn left through this to quickly arrive at the tiny tarn of Llyn y Wrach. Pass this on its right-hand side and follow the path down a shallow valley to reach the power lines followed on the outward leg. Turn right and follow them back to the car.

Tal y Fan summit

WALK 2

Aber Falls and the Northern Carneddau

Start/Finish	Bont Newydd, Abergwyngregyn SH 662 720
Distance	20km (12½ miles)
Total ascent	1020m (3350ft)
Grade	Strenuous
Time	7hr
Terrain	Mainly good paths with a couple of trackless and boggy sections
Map	OS OL17 Snowdon/Yr Wyddfa
Access	Abergwyngregyn is reached by the A55 from Bangor to Conwy: follow signs from the village to Aber Falls
Parking	Pay and display parking at Bont Newydd
Note	The Northern Carneddau are even less trodden than the southern summits in the group. This walk covers consistently high ground, much of it on largely featureless slopes which demand good navigation in mist.

Aber Falls are deservedly popular with visitors to the North Wales coast. The combination of easy access and a spectacular waterfall where the Afon Goch plunges 37m (120ft) down the rock face proves an irresistible combination, but the broad smooth path to the falls should not fool walkers into thinking this is going to be a stroll. Once the falls are left behind the atmosphere changes dramatically and it becomes a taxing expedition.

From the bridge turn right opposite a little cottage into an overspill car park and picnic area, following signs to the falls. The path winds up through a pleasant wooded valley on a wide, firm track. There is a slightly rougher diversion through the woods, but with so much walking ahead it seems a little early to go looking for trouble.

Either path eventually brings you the **Aber Falls**, a sleek white ribbon running down the face. It feels a

little early for a stop but this is a sight to be savoured. When you have admired the falls enough take a foot-bridge across the stream and carry on up the path beyond as it contours round to reach **Rhaeadr bach** ('the small falls'). ▶

About 100 metres or so further down the path by a small tree on the left hand side take a narrow path through the bracken up to the fence line, which is fol-lowed rightwards to a small stile giving onto the open hillside. Follow the track diagonally rightwards to cross the stream and continue up the slope. There is no point pretending this next section is anything but toil as the path plays hide and seek in the bracken appearing and then vanishing only to re-emerge 30 metres higher up so wide that you cannot imagine how you lost it. Eventually the angle relents and the path becomes clearer as it deliv-ers you onto the often-soggy col between **Moel Wnion** and Drosgl.

Carry on across it to reach a path between the two hills and turn left to begin the climb up **Drosgl**. As the ground begins to slope upwards a vehicle track, the best you have seen for well over an hour, appears. However,

The sleek white ribbon of Aber Falls

It's a shame to encounter these falls second, as without the presence of their larger companion just round the corner they would feel rather more impressive.

29

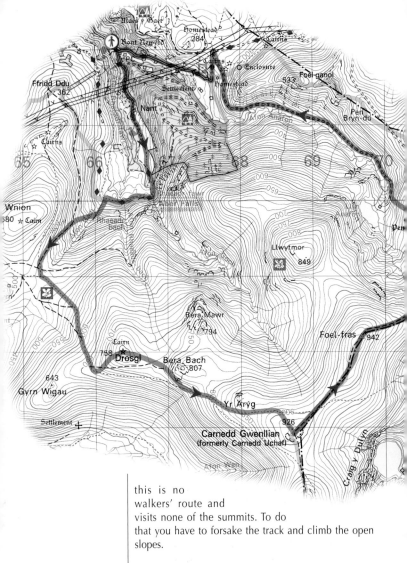

this is no
walkers' route and
visits none of the summits. To do
that you have to forsake the track and climb the open
slopes.

The rounded, grassy summit of **Drosgl** holds a last
minute surprise, a vast mound of stones which is

said to be a Bronze Age burial cairn. Certainly it represents a huge effort on someone's part.

From the summit, looking eastwards, the twin rocky tors of Bera Mawr and Bera Bach are visible across a shallow depression. The shapely cone of **Bera Bach** is our next objective: it is soon reached, and proves to be a shattered pyramid. From it carry on over the largely pathless jumble of boulders interspersed with broad stretches of grass where your only companions are likely to be sheep and the semi-wild mountain ponies which roam here. The next target is another rocky knoll, **Yr Aryg**, at the top of the next slope, which is passed on its right to press on to the next pile of stones on top of **Carnedd Uchaf**, which has recently undergone a double promotion, having been elevated by a re-survey to the Welsh 3000ft club and given a second name, **Carnedd Gwenllian**.

The new name Gwenllian commemorates the daughter of **Llewelyn, the last Prince of Wales**. Her mother, who is commemorated in the name of Yr Elen, died in childbirth and shortly afterwards her father was killed in battle and her uncle Dafydd captured and executed. King Edward I of England saw his chance to snuff out the Welsh royal line and imprisoned her in convents for the rest of her days. The elevation of the peak to a separate 3000ft summit (as shown on the latest maps) has caused controversy among long distance walkers and fell runners since it has added an extra top to the long-established classic round of the Welsh 3000s, playing havoc with the record books.

From here everything is about to change once more. As you leave the summit rocks you quickly reach the main north-south path which traverses the spine of the Carneddau. Here things become a little busier and the

Ponies on descent from Drum

paths easier to follow although the day's work is far from over as you press on along the rocky track to **Foel-fras**, at 942m (3089ft) the highest point of the day.

From here there is a long grassy descent and climb northwards to **Drum**, with its summit cairn safely tucked away behind the fence. Following the main track would eventually bring you back to Pont Newydd but instead, from the summit, cross the path and head off down the steep grass slope aiming for the access track of **Llyn Anafon** directly below. There is the faintest of green paths which I have sometimes stumbled across and sometimes not: it is so vague that I suspect it moves about over time and down the years I have learned to treat its occasional appearances as something of a bonus rather than anything to be expected.

At the end of a fairly long day this beautiful, lonely valley is a delight to walk with the going underfoot easy and all navigation problems at an end: admire the views of the heather-covered hillside and enjoy the company of the mountain ponies grazing beside the lively stream which emerges from the reservoir, until the track reaches the road which is followed back to the car park.

WALK 3
Cwm Eigiau Horseshoe

Start/Finish	Parking area in Cwm Eigiau SH 733 664
Distance	16km (10 miles)
Total ascent	1075m (3525ft)
Grade	Strenuous
Time	6–7hr
Terrain	Untracked hillside, steep ridges and tracks; brief easy scramble
Map	OS OL17 Snowdon/Yr Wyddfa
Access	Take the B5106 to Tal-y-Bont in the Conwy Valley and turn left on an unmarked lane 100 metres south of the Y Bedol pub (note: this is **not** the road next to the pub signed to Llanbedr-y-Cennin). The single track road leads steeply uphill and at a junction carry straight on. The road, which has several gates, ends after a little over 5km (3 miles) at a small parking area by a locked gate.
Parking	By the locked gate
Note	Leaving Foel Grach involves crossing an untracked and featureless hillside aiming for a grass track. It would be very easy to go wrong here so the walk is best avoided in bad visibility or if there is a likelihood of low cloud.

Although they contain a cluster of summits over the magic 3000ft mark the Carneddau are remarkably quiet compared with the Glyderau on the other side of the Ogwen Valley or the Snowdon massif. This is especially true of the deep valleys below the main north–south ridge, and nowhere more so than in the broad basin of Cwm Eigiau. Here, even on days when Snowdon is groaning under the weight of school parties and Three Peakers, it is possible to have entire mountains to yourself. Driving along the narrow lane from Tal-y-Bont it is impossible not to be affected by the lonely sweep of this once bustling valley and its overwhelming emptiness.

From the parking area much of the walk remains hidden beyond the curve of Cwm Eigiau but it is possible to weigh up the first objective, Pen Llithrig y Wrach ('The Slippery Head of the Witch').

Who the **witch** was and why her head should be slippery has been lost in the mists of time. Asked the story behind the name, a local farmer shrugged and admitted he was baffled.

The walk starts in friendly enough fashion, crossing a ladder stile beside the locked gate and striding out easily along the continuation of the road which runs up to a huge wall. This proves to be the breached dam of the ill-fated **Llyn Eigiau Reservoir**. ◀

In 1925 the dam failed and 16 people were drowned in the resulting flood.

The road passes below the dam and then up to the whitewashed cottage of

34

Hafod-y-rhiw, which must be one of the most isolated houses in Wales. Beyond the house the track almost immediately vanishes and becomes as tricky as the first stretch was easy, as the witch decides to test her suitors. This is perhaps the toughest part of the whole walk, climbing through ankle-snagging heather and rushes. Paths whimsically appear and then just as quickly vanish, waxing and waning without apparent rhyme or reason. The general line is a leftward slanting valley taking you below the line of outcrops at the top of the slope. Having passed these the various paths coalesce into a single grassy track weaving between rocky knolls, craglets and mini-gullies to arrive on a bald subsidiary top. Happily, the worst is now over but there is still a long way to go, crossing a couple of boggy cols before climbing the final grassy slope to the summit of **Pen Llithrig y Wrach**.

On the final approach it is possible to look down to the left on **Llyn Cowlyd**, reputed to be the deepest lake in Wales at more than 70m (230ft), with the unmistakeable shape of Tryfan and the Glyderau

Cwm Eigiau's breached dam

beyond and Snowdon peeping over their shoulders. Ahead the giants of the Carneddau beckon you on.

In all, the ascent to the comparatively lowly summit at 799m (2297ft) that seemed so innocuous from the car park will probably have consumed a couple of hours or more.

Having worked so hard for the summit, the ridge to the next top, Pen yr Helgi Du, only a little higher at 833m (2732ft), involves a frustratingly long descent of more than 160m (525ft) to the **Bwlch y Tri Marchog** ('the pass of the three horsemen'), another intriguing name: but sadly, like the witch, the riders have also been forgotten. Beyond it is the grassy shoulder of Pen yr Helgi Du and a 200m (660ft) climb, while further along the ridge are the vast plunging buttresses of Craig yr Ysfa, which might have been placed there deliberately to give the lie to the old accusation that the Carneddau are just grassy lumps.

Once over the broad summit of **Pen yr Helgi Du**, with its slightly misplaced cairn, the character of the walk changes markedly. The ridge ahead becomes narrow and exposed, with a steep drop down into **Cwm Eigiau** to the right and **Flynnon Llugwy Reservoir** to the left, while ahead the ridge plunges steeply to a saddle which proves much easier than it looks from above.

Beyond the col the path carries on up the narrow crest and provides a brief easy scramble through a band of slabs before traversing above **Craig yr Ysfa** onto a broader slope. It arrives on the very summit of **Carnedd Llewelyn**, although this is not immediately clear as the top is a huge stony plateau.

Turn right, heading northwards along the main Carneddau ridge, dropping down a stony slope to a col and then a rather smoother climb over grass to the 976m (3201ft) summit rocks of **Foel Grach**.

Leftwards across Cwm Caseg, the **view from Foel Grach** is dominated by Yr Elen's huge shattered face. Just behind and below the summit of Foel Grach is a **rudimentary bothy** intended to be an emergency refuge for those caught out by darkness or bad weather on these otherwise shelterless tops.

In good visibility the descent from here is clear, despite the lack of obvious paths. ▶ The general aim is to reach the ridge on the north western side of Cwm Eigiau. A clear track can be seen traversing the side of the ridge but this is used only in its very lowest section.

Head off south eastwards across mostly trackless grass, where any footprints you come across are likely to be left by the horseshoes of the semi-wild ponies that graze here rather than the cleated rubber of walkers. Work your way across the slope, aiming for the ridge, and eventually the reservoir of **Melynllyn** comes into view below. Shortly afterwards the contouring path intersects a broad track running along the ridge. Carry on down this and where it passes to the left of a cockscomb of rocky outcrops the valley's second lake, **Dulyn Reservoir** appears in a dark, crag-girt hollow. The path, now much narrower, begins to descend more steeply across the slope, eventually dropping to join the access track by a gate. Go through this and follow the broad track as it curls round the end of the ridge to descend to the car park.

In mist or darkness it is a very tricky exercise in navigation and best avoided.

Near the summit of Carnedd Llewelyn

37

WALK 4
The Southern Carneddau

Start/Finish	Llyn Ogwen on A5 between Capel Curig and Bethesda SH 648 604
Distance	16km (10 miles)
Total ascent	1170m (3840ft)
Grade	Strenuous
Time	6hr
Terrain	Steep climb followed by stony ridges; simple scrambling
Map	OS OL17 Snowdon/Yr Wyddfa
Access	Llyn Ogwen is on A5 between Capel Curig and Bethesda
Parking	Pay and display car park by Llyn Ogwen or free spaces by the road

The Carneddau have a reputation in some circles of being a bit tame and even perhaps a little boring. Looking from the shores of Llyn Ogwen it's an easy mistake to make, especially when you contrast their green slopes with the rocky turrets of Tryfan or the deep clefts and cwms of the Glyderau on the other side of the valley. But don't be fooled. Hidden within their folds the Carneddau harbour dramatic cwms and huge cliffs. Their rounded tops have often been compared with Scotland's Cairngorms, and when winter gales scour the ridges they can feel every bit as wild. These are not mountains to be underestimated and several of the summits top the magic 3000ft contour. This walk visits three of them, Pen yr Ole Wen, Carnedd Dafydd and Carnedd Llewelyn, in a glorious high round.

It is possible to make a direct assault on Pen yr Ole Wen by a path which hurls itself directly at the ridge rising from the western end of Llyn Ogwen, but this is a brutally steep choice best left to masochists and would-be SAS candidates. This easier and more devious route climbs easily into lovely Cwm Lloer and throws in an easy scramble to ease the height gain.

Walk east along the A5 towards Capel Curig and turn left at the first lane beyond the lake towards **Tal y Llyn** Farm, passing the MAM climbing hut at Glan Dena. Just before reaching the farm gate take a pitched path heading up the hillside. This climbs beside the **Afon Lloer**, paved in places but quite wet in others, until it reaches the rim of Cwm Lloer. From here it turns leftwards up the fine enclosing ridge, which provides a simple scramble with impressive views back across the valley to the stern North Ridge of Tryfan and the rocky faces of the Glyderau.

The top of the scramble proves not to be the top of the hill, and the path continues around the rim of the cwm to the bare

summit of **Pen yr Ole Wen**. Once this has been reached the hardest work has been done, and what remains is top quality ridge walking where it is possible to stride out and gobble up the miles.

The track now curves away around the cwm, staying well away from the edge and crossing the minor top of **Carnedd Fach**, traversing a wilderness of stones relieved only by patches of Alpine grasses and mosses. The top of **Carnedd Dafydd**, perhaps not surprisingly, given the wealth of building material available on all sides, is crowned with a sprawling cairn and commodious wind-breaks. From here the broad track carries on around the ridge towards Carnedd Llewelyn.

As you circle the cwm **the Carneddau** begin to reveal their true character, with deeply scalloped hollows cradling secret lakes and a surprising amount of naked rock worthy of any mountain lover's attention.

The path stretches away along the largely featureless ridge before taking a distinct dogleg to the north to begin the climb of the final slopes of **Carnedd Llewelyn**, a great shivering pile of stones. The path arrives on the edge of the summit plateau by a windbreak. ▸

This is a crucial landmark for the descent.

Glancing round the summit reveals it to be decorated with a large number of rocky protuberances, any one of which might be **the actual summit**. With no trig point to settle the argument there is little for it but to check for yourself and at the end of your investigations you may well come to the conclusion that it is by the windbreak after all.

From here take what would have been a right turn on your arrival, heading south east towards the summit of Pen yr Helgi Du. The start is marked with a large cairn a few metres down the hill. The path drops steeply down and as it nears the col it passes above the climbing crag of **Craig yr Ysfa** down to the left. This is followed by a short section where it is necessary to clamber down rocks to reach the col, with the reservoir of **Ffynnon Llugwy** below to the right.

Descent from Carnedd Llewelyn to Pen yr Helgi Du

41

From the bald sheep-cropped summit there is a satisfying panorama of virtually the entire day's route.

The ridge to **Pen yr Helgi Du** provides an enjoyable finale to the walk ◄

Shortcut missing out Pen yr Helgi Du
For those without the energy to spare for a final summit, the quickest and most direct descent takes a path from the far end of the col which drops steeply down to the reservoir, passing it on its left hand side to reach the access road which is followed to the A5.

From the summit of Pen yr Helgi Du turn right (south) down the broad grassy ridge which provides welcome relief for the knees and feet on springy turf after all the miles of stones. As it nears the A5 the path jinks to the right of some buildings and drops down to the access track. Follow this down to the main road.

> The tiny building opposite is **Helyg**, a mountaineering hut owned by the Climbers' Club, and a spot which has played a pivotal role in mountaineering both in Snowdonia and elsewhere. It was a temporary home to many of the early rock climbing pioneers when the sport was being developed in Wales and was also used as a training base by members of the 1953 Everest expedition before they left for Nepal to make the first ascent of the world's highest mountain.

Cross the road to a ladder stile and take the path heading across the valley floor. At a stile and a T-junction where it reaches a broader track, the old road from Capel Curig before the present A5 was built, turn right for a pleasant traffic-free couple of miles back to **Llyn Ogwen**.

WALK 5

Cwm Llafar Horseshoe

Start/Finish	Gerlan, Bethesda SH 634 664
Distance	16km (10 miles)
Total ascent	1020m (3350ft)
Grade	Strenuous
Time	5–6hr
Terrain	Grassy slopes and intermittent paths
Map	OS OL17 Snowdon/Yr Wyddfa
Access	From Bethesda turn uphill almost opposite the large and impressive central chapel. Turn right at a mini-roundabout a few metres up the hill and carry on into Ffordd Gerlan.
Parking	Roadside in Gerlan or free in Bethesda. Gerlan is a small community of narrow lanes and parking spaces are at a premium: take care not to block access or passing spaces. If nothing is available park in one of several free car parks in Bethesda and walk up.

The eastern approach to the highest of the Carneddau tops is in complete contrast to the approach from Ogwen in Walk 4. While the ascent over Pen yr Ole Wen is taken by thousands, this route is walked by only a handful. The tracks are narrow and in places faint or even non-existent, while the overall feel is much wilder and more remote than the approach from Nant Ffrancon.

Walk out of Gerlan on its narrow main street, which quickly becomes an even narrower, tree-lined lane heading towards the mountains. At the end of the tarmac this comes to a house named Ty Dwr and a sign reading 'private road'. This is, however, a public footpath. Go up this and take a stile to the right of the house gates. Carry on up the left hand side of the field to another stile by a gate almost in the top left hand corner. Go over this and carry on towards the mountains, as directed by a series of way-markers and ladder stiles to the edge of open country.

Although the walk has started from the streets of Bethesda and the village is still visible behind, this feels like an **altogether more remote landscape** than the bustling paths of the Glyderau just a few miles up the A5. This may be because of the bare hills grazed by cattle and sheep or the neglected look of the often wet fields, which are running to sour grasses, rushes and bracken.

Ahead the horseshoe is now taking shape, with the grassy tongue of **Mynydd Du** rising towards Carnedd Dafydd and the rim of the cwm curling round rightwards to Carnedd Llewelyn and Yr Elen.

Just after reaching an incongruous ruined enclosure with concrete posts and iron railings the path carries on into the cwm, but for the horseshoe it

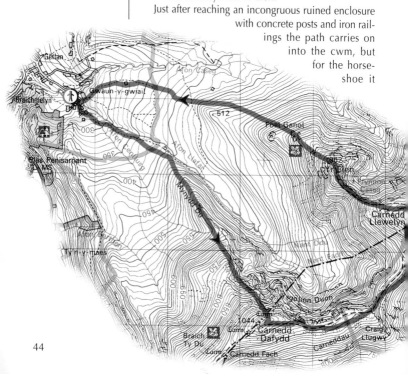

is necessary to take a narrower path which breaks away rightwards up the enclosing ridge. The grassy path attacks the slope head-on before offering a brief respite on a level section perched on the edge of the steep-sided cwm with views down to the now unfashionable climbers' crag of Llech Du below, with the shattered crags of the Black Ladders beyond.

There is little to amuse the summer rock climber on the Ladders, but in winter when the loose rock is frozen into place it offers some of the most challenging **ice climbing** in Snowdonia.

The final pull to the summit of **Carnedd Dafydd** is through large boulders interspersed with grass and bilberries.

At **Carnedd Dafydd's summit** is a windbreak, which offers tremendous views particularly across to Snowdon, the Glyderau and Tryfan to the south while to north the dogleg ridge curls round Cwm Llafar to Carnedd Llewelyn.

Carry on circling the rim of the cwm, with the Black Ladders now below and on past rocky knolls and the col of Bwlch Cyfryw-drum to climb the long stony slope to arrive at the summit windbreak of **Carnedd Llewelyn** perched on the eastern rim of the plateau. From here the next summit, Yr Elen, is out of sight and it is necessary to cross to the western rim where the linking path becomes apparent.

As you descend the slope and cross a small lip there is a jaw-dropping moment as the huge east face of **Yr Elen** makes a theatrical appearance, unsuspected and unannounced. The great shattered slope, bounded by the sharp rocks of the south east arête and the narrow path clinging to its side, drops away hundreds of metres into Cwm Caseg far below. It is as fine a sight as is to be found anywhere in Snowdonia and this is a very special moment and made all the better for its dramatic suddenness. Never again let anyone try to tell you that the Carneddau are just boring, rounded grassy lumps.

◄ The first part of the descent from Yr Elen takes you down a steep eroded scree slope that gives way to springy turf leading down the general line of the ridge with the rooftops of Bethesda beyond.

The final section is tricky to follow, with the path weaving through rushes and becoming intertwined with sheep paths which can lead you astray, but with the houses of Bethesda ahead and the occasional marker post and footpath sign to guide you the lane used on the outward leg is finally reached.

The summit of Yr Elen, named after the wife of Llewelyn, is a fine isolated top from which to survey the central ridge of the Carneddau.

The fine isolated top of Yr Elen

THE GLYDERAU

Cwm Idwal (Walk 11)

WALK 6

Gallt yr Ogof and Y Foel Goch

Start/Finish	Capel Curig SH 721 582
Distance	14km (9 miles)
Total ascent	670m (2198ft)
Grade	Moderate
Time	5hr
Terrain	An often wet ridge and rough descent in Cwm Tryfan
Map	OS OL17 Snowdon/Yr Wyddfa
Access	Capel Curig is on the A5 between Betws-y-Coed and Ogwen
Parking	National park car park car park behind Joe Brown's outdoor shop by the junction with the A4086

Gallt yr Ogof is a striking mountain that not many people remember. It is an imposing enough presence driving north west on the A5, a great bruiser of a hill that fills the windscreen: it is neither elegant nor subtle but it is utterly ignorable. The problem is the company it keeps. Many a traveller will have admired its vast, rugged flank studded with rocks and shattered buttresses only to instantly forget it as the even more imposing ridges of Tryfan come into view. It would be a rare hill that could compete with that. So Gallt yr Ogof and its neighbour Y Foel Goch stand largely ignored by most visitors to the Ogwen, and that is a shame: together they provide not only the emphatic eastern full stop to the extended ridge of the Glyderau but also offer a perfect viewpoint for their more illustrious neighbours and beyond.

From the car park turn right up the lane away from the village and after a couple of hundred metres at a gate by a farm take the path heading up leftwards through the outcrops and bracken. As it reaches the crest the views begin to open out. To the left Moel Siabod has been a companion for much of the ascent, but now the whole of the Snowdon Horseshoe is revealed while on the other side of the valley the eastern Carneddau begin to appear.

Looking towards Gallt yr Ogof

Indeed the views are perhaps one of the strongest attractions of this high level promenade and a particularly welcome feature of this next section. ▶

At the end of the plateau the path climbs the grassy slope, crossing a drystone wall by a ladder stile before being funnelled between a tumbledown wall and a more modern wire fence as it heads towards the skyline. In its haste to reach the higher tops of the Glyderau the main path actually bypasses the 763m (2503ft) summit of **Gallt yr Ogof**.

As the path arrives on the rim of the Ogwen Valley Tryfan makes a dramatic entrance befitting its starring role, leaping into view between a gap in the knolls, quickly to be joined by the Glyderau themselves and the spiky profile of Bristly Ridge is seen to particularly good effect, silhouetted against the skyline.

Having stopped to admire the huge buttresses, it is necessary to backtrack a short way eastwards to visit the

Were it not for the views this long, flat, often soggy ridge might otherwise make for an uninspiring interlude.

Tryfan and the Glyders from Gallt yr Ogof

summit cairn of Gallt yr Ogof sitting among the boulders on a rocky plinth.

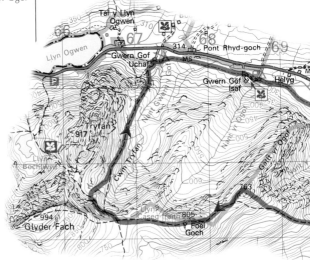

After the long haul to the first summit of the day the second demands only the simplest and briefest of strolls, returning to the ridge path and crossing the shallow col, skirting to the right of some marshy pools before the easy walk to the 805m (2641ft) summit of **Y Foel Goch**.

This is yet another ideal spot from which to enjoy the **unfolding panorama**, taking in the whole of the Snowdon Horseshoe, the Glyderau, Nant Gwynant and the distant sea, the crags of Tryfan and the giants of the Carneddau.

From Y Foel Goch the track drops down to the small collection of tarns of **Llyn Caseg-fraith** in another damp col. Just beyond the pools is the old Miners' Track. ▶

This track was used each week by men to walk from Bethesda and Ogwen to reach their toil in the slate mines and quarries of Snowdon.

From here it would be simple to extend the walk over the main Glyderau themselves and onwards even to Y Garn using Walks 7 and 11 to return via Ogwen, but if these higher tops are to be the day's main objective there are much better and more exciting approaches than this one.

After passing Llyn Caseg-fraith keep leftwards close to the rim of the valley, where there is a good and relatively dry path. Follow this until it starts to climb and comes to a substantial cairn which marks the junction with the Miners' Track coming up from Bwlch Tryfan. Turn right down

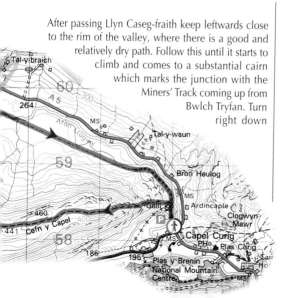

this, taking care on the upper section which is steep and badly eroded. It winds downhill before beginning a long traverse across the slope towards Bwlch Tryfan on the other side of **Cwm Tryfan**. Before reaching the col, several small and not terribly inviting paths drop down the scree but the easiest way is to traverse almost as far as to where the path begins to rise towards the col and a clearer, though still quite rough, path turns down the valley. Follow this, working your way down below the huge crags until it eventually joins a pitched path which passes behind the climbers' slabs of Tryfan Bach to reach a farm almost in the valley bottom.

> The farm buildings stand beside a broad gravel track which was once part of the **old coach road** from Ogwen to Capel Curig and was the main valley route until it was superseded by Thomas Telford's A5.

Turn right along this for the long but straightforward return to Capel Curig, passing through farms and a campsite, the miles enlivened by a very different view of Gallt yr Ogof's rugged face.

Extension

If you have been tempted to extend the walk over the Glyderau it will be necessary to walk back up the A5 to the eastern end of Llyn Ogwen and then a little further up the road to where, almost opposite the turn off to Glan Dena, the old coach road, signed to Capel Curig, turns off rightwards.

WALK 7

Glyderau from Pen-y-Gwryd

Start/Finish	Pen-y-Gwryd Hotel on A4086 5km west of Capel Curig SH 662 559
Distance	10km (6 miles)
Total ascent	804m (2613ft)
Grade	Moderate
Time	4–5hr
Terrain	Hill tracks, wet in places; easy scrambles
Map	OS OL17 Snowdon/Yr Wyddfa
Access	On the A4086 between Capel Curig and Beddgelert
Parking	Pay and display in layby near hotel; free parking further along the A4086 towards Capel Curig

There is no denying that the Glyderau present their most exciting face to the north where a line of deeply sculpted cwms and massive crags loom over the Ogwen Valley but that does not mean the southern slopes should be ignored. They have plenty of interest of their own, including rocky ridges with easy scrambles, a hidden lake and, perhaps best of all, solitude on days when the northern slopes are besieged by visitors. They also have the advantage of starting from higher up for their assault on this pair of giants, Glyder Fawr at 999m (3279ft) and little brother Glyder Fach at 994m (3262ft). There are also some exceptional views of the Snowdon massif both on the ascent and on the return leg, so save this circuit for a clear day to see it at its very best.

This walk starts from the **Pen-y-Gwryd Hotel** at the junction of the Capel Curig to Beddgelert road and the A4086, which climbs over Pen-y-Pass to Llanberis. The hotel has a proud place in the history of British climbing, playing host to some of the earliest pioneers of Welsh mountaineering and rock climbing as well as to members of the successful 1953 expedition which first climbed Mount Everest.

From the layby walk past the hotel and across the road junction for about 150 metres and take a path on the right signed to Pen-y-Pass. ◄

This is a much more agreeable route than walking directly up the road and is considerably safer.

At Pen-y-Pass car park turn your back on the crowds heading for Snowdon and cross the road to take a ladder stile immediately to the left of the youth hostel to follow the path as it climbs away diagonally leftwards. From the very beginning the views back to Snowdon, and especially Crib Goch, are superb and only get better as height is gained.

The path, guided by the occasional splodge of red paint, leads over a rise to reveal the wild hollow cradling **Llyn Cwmffynnon**. Keep well to the left of the lake and stay as high as possible to avoid the worst of the marshy ground before beginning to attack the rocky spur.

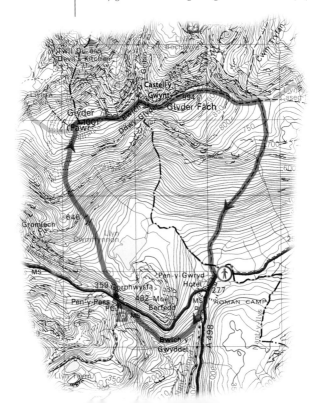

Pen-y-Gwryd Hotel

Although there are plenty of small crags in evidence and it is easy to concoct an entertaining series of scrambles, the main path weaves easily through them. Eventually after more than an hour's steady climbing the summit ridges of the Glyderau come into view and the angle begins to ease. The path climbs through a final band of scree to reach the ridge, a rocky wilderness of boulders and rock fangs.

Turn right to reach the summit of **Glyder Fawr**, with extensive views along the rest of the range, out to the sea and northwards to the Carneddau, which join the Snowdon tops in the panorama. From the summit carry on eastwards aiming for the blocky pyramid of Glyder Fach, Glyder Fawr's littler brother a mile away and only a paltry 5m lower. The path is rocky but marked by the scuffing of countless boots and the occasional cairn.

As the plateau's boulder field is left behind the path becomes easier to follow and as you drop into the dip between the two Glyder summits the landmark of the **Castell y Gwynt** ('Castle of the Winds') begins to emerge from the rocky grey background and is revealed as a collection of freestanding pinnacles and huge shards of rock perched on the very edge of the abyss dropping down into Cwm Bochlwyd. Pass the Castell either via a gap just

55

Approaching Castell y Gwynt

below and to the right its summit or by diverting along a path which skirts even further below it to the right. The jumbled rocks of the summit of **Glyder Fach** are just beyond.

From the summit carry on in much the same easterly line along the rim of the northern slopes but be careful not to be lured down onto the scramble of Bristly Ridge coming up from Cwm Tryfan nor by the scree chute coming up its flank. The junction is marked by a large cairn. Instead clamber through a wide gap in the rocks to the east which reveals the path heading away down the slope towards the distant pool of **Llyn Caseg-fraith**.

Drop down towards the llyn but before reaching it a cairn marks the point where the Miners' Track comes up from the left from Bwlch Tryfan and another cairn to the right marks its continuation across the moor. Turn rightwards along this, crossing a boggy section, before starting downhill by a rocky tor where it turns right and the **Pen-y-Gwryd Hotel** and its eponymous lake appear in the valley below. Follow the path down towards the hotel, with yet more fine views into the Snowdon Horseshoe and southwards down Nantgwynant, to cross a footbridge and reach the road.

WALK 8

Tryfan by the North Ridge and Heather Terrace

Start/Finish	Layby beneath Milestone Buttress SH 663 603
Distance	6km (4 miles)
Total ascent	614m (2014ft)
Grade	Strenuous, Grade 1 scramble
Time	3–4hr
Terrain	Steep rock ridge followed by an exposed path
Map	OS OL17 Snowdon/Yr Wyddfa
Access	On A5 by Llyn Ogwen between Bethesda and Capel Curig
Parking	Layby beneath the Milestone Buttress
Note	The North Ridge, while never desperate, demands a steady head and some route finding ability. The easiest line seldom strays far from the crest and most of the difficulties can be outflanked quite easily. Add snow, ice, damp rock or high winds and it becomes a much more serious proposition demanding specialist equipment and the knowledge of how to use it.

At 3002ft (915m), Tryfan scrapes into the magic 3000ft club. But even if it did not it would still be Snowdonia's most eye-catching mountain, stealing the show in any view in which it appears. Driving up the A5 from Bethesda it smacks you in the eye, a great wall of rock filling the windscreen. Coming the other way from Capel Curig the vast pyramid, crowned by its triple summits with steep ridges on either end, looks like something transplanted from the Italian Dolomites. Seen end on, from Glyder Fach or the high Carneddau, it is a slender stone steeple. It is a mountain that impresses from every angle and cries out to be climbed. Tryfan does not surrender its summit easily: no one strolls up it with their hands in their pockets. The flanks are the province of the rock climber, but the two ridges yield to the scrambler, offering wonderful adventure without demanding too much in return, save effort and a modicum of sweat. But as recompense Tryfan will afford you some of the best days of your walking life.

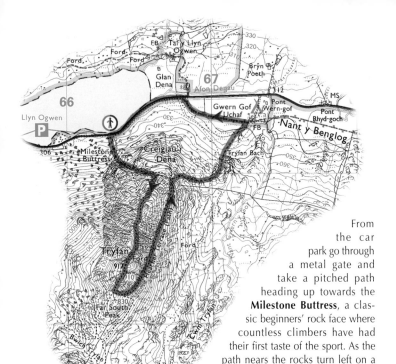

map at 1:25,000 scale

This is the start of the scrambling, initially up more boulders and through broken rock which is marked in the most popular places by the passage of many feet and hands.

From the car park go through a metal gate and take a pitched path heading up towards the **Milestone Buttress**, a classic beginners' rock face where countless climbers have had their first taste of the sport. As the path nears the rocks turn left on a steadily less-manicured track which rises steeply across the slope. The path becomes a little harder to follow when it reaches a boulder field but the most trodden route tends to stay close to the foot of the crags. Eventually it crests the North Ridge by a large cairn on a boulder. ◄

The route climbs steadily, weaving to and fro but seldom straying far from the crest. Those who want a more entertaining ascent will find plenty of short rock steps to amuse them to either side. As it climbs higher the path reaches a flatter area above which the tricky sections become a little harder to avoid. The path also passes a projecting stone, The Cannon, which looks as though it is about fire a salute over Ogwen.

The final tower, whose foot is marked by a large cairn, looks especially daunting, but its bark is much worse than its bite. It can be outflanked by a path which

descends from the cairn through a gap in the rock and then bypasses the tower to its left. The final obstacle is a tricky little descent into a gap, but a little exploration should reveal the easiest route. From here carry on to the central summit of **Tryfan**.

Tryfan North Ridge and Llyn Ogwen

> Tryfan's summit is unmistakeable thanks to a pair of flat-topped pinnacles known as **Adam and Eve**. Which one is Adam and which is Eve is a matter of much conjecture and little importance. You may find one or other occupied by a young man – it's almost always a young man – who has clambered up to make the traditional leap from one to the other to impress his (usually female) companions. However, having belatedly discovered that it is both further and higher than he thought, he will now be desperately thinking of a way to extricate himself without either a) losing face or b) breaking his neck.

Carry on over the south summit and begin to descend the south ridge. Although easier than the North Ridge, this still requires care and a little hand and foot work as well as attentive route finding. In most cases the easiest

Adam and Eve on Tryfan's summit

way is off to the right. At the bottom of the slope is a ladder stile over a wall just before a final rocky island above Bwlch Tryfan, which separates the mountain from Glyder Fach's Bristly Ridge (see Walk 10).

Cross the stile and drop down a steep, eroded scree chute for about 75m (250ft) to a large cairn on the left hand side of the gully by a large triangular boulder. This marks the start of **Heather Terrace**, an unlikely narrow trod which crosses the face just below the foot of the climbers' crags.

The track initially climbs a few feet before beginning its undulating, but generally downward progress as an airy catwalk high above **Cwm Tryfan**. At one point the path loses itself among rocks, but carry on in the same line and it soon reappears slowly dropping down the flank of the mountain. When it is almost level with the triangular climbing slabs of **Tryfan Bach** ('Little Tryfan'), another novices' crag on the other side of the valley, the path descends some steep steps in a narrow cleft to emerge on the open hillside and moves way from Tryfan to meet a broader path coming down the valley, which it joins to pass Tryfan Bach and carry on down to a farm. Turn left along the broad track and follow it to the road. Turn left again for a few hundred metres to reach the car.

WALK 9

Tryfan Without Fears

Start/Finish	Layby beneath Milestone Buttress SH 663 603
Distance	6.5km (4 miles)
Total ascent	614m (2014ft)
Grade	Moderate with easy scrambling
Time	3–4hr
Terrain	A slightly exposed traverse and mountain paths
Map	OS OL17 Snowdon/Yr Wyddfa
Access	On A5 by Llyn Ogwen between Bethesda and Capel Curig
Parking	Layby beneath the Milestone Buttress, and see below
Note	There is no absolutely simple way up Tryfan – it's not that sort of mountain – but this is the least difficult, while still retaining some of the atmosphere and excitement which make Tryfan such an attractive summit. As with all scrambling, this assumes an ascent in good, dry conditions. Under snow and ice, on damp rock or even in high winds it becomes a much more serious proposition demanding specialist equipment and the knowledge of how to use it.

To any red-blooded walker Tryfan is quite simply the must-do mountain of the Ogwen Valley and even perhaps of all Snowdonia. From every angle it presents naked rock, two vast faces and two superb ridges. But what sets one person's pulse racing may set another's knees quaking. The finest way up is the North Ridge (as described in Walk 8), but if that looks too daunting there are alternatives. The simplest would be to take the Cwm Tryfan path up the eastern side and then the easiest way up the path on the South Ridge, but unless you have absolutely no head for heights that is to short change yourself.

This route takes the startling-looking yet fairly straightforward rising traverse of Heather Terrace, which cuts across the east face and retains at least some of the special atmosphere of Tryfan with few of the associated worries. Using the Heather Terrace as an ascent route rather than as a way down has the other advantage that it is rather easier to find from below than above. The only real drawback of this route is that it does involve some unavoidable road walking beside the A5. I have suggested parking by the Milestone Buttress, but any of the car parks and laybys between Ogwen Cottage and Glan Dena at the eastern end of Llyn Ogwen would work just as well.

From the car park walk eastwards along the A5 to the end of **Llyn Ogwen**, and then take a track on the right signed to Capel Curig. Follow this broad track for a few hundred metres as far as the farm at **Gwern Gof Uchaf**. Go through the gate on the main track beside the farm and then immediately take a stile on the right to follow a paved path which climbs up to pass beneath the face of **Tryfan Bach** ('Little Tryfan'). ◀ Continue uphill until the path reaches a ladder stile on a wall. Do not go over but

Tryfan Bach is an easy angled slab used for teaching novice climbers.

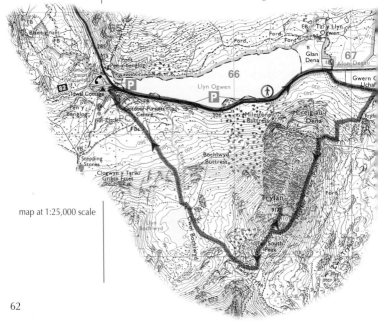

map at 1:25,000 scale

Tryfan with Heather Terrace cutting below the crags

instead turn right to follow a smaller path across the hillside and up through a narrow cleft with steps built into it.

At the top turn left on the narrow path. This is the start of **Heather Terrace**, a tremendous route which takes you into some breathtaking situations high above the valley and directly beneath the climbers' crags without ever placing any great strain on nerves. It slowly climbs across the face to eventually arrive in a steep scree gully, easily the most unpleasant part of the route. Clamber up this for about 75m (250ft) to reach a col with a ladder stile. Go over this and then begin the ascent of the south ridge. This does involve some simple scrambling but you can make it as hard or as easy as you wish by the choice of route. When in doubt the easiest way is usually to the left. The ridge takes you over the south summit to the main top of **Tryfan** which is easily identified by two pillars, Adam and Eve.

63

Tryfan's south ridge: its bark is worse than its bite

To descend, retrace your steps as far as the ladder stile above the Heather Terrace then continue down the ridge, skirting the rock island on its right to reach another col, **Bwlch Tryfan**. The descent to the left would take you down into Cwm Tryfan and the road but instead take the right hand path, which leads down to the shore of **Llyn Bochlwyd**, a beautiful sheet of water dramatically cradled between the faces of Tryfan, Glyder Fach and Y Gribin. Take the path along the eastern side of the lake to the head of the stream which plunges into the lower cwm. The path soon fords this on boulders and then continues beside it. ◀

Along the stream is a series of attractive waterfalls and cascades.

As it approaches the valley floor the path joins the main pitched path coming down from **Llyn Idwal**. Turn right along it and within a few minutes reach the café and information centre by Ogwen Cottage. Turn right back along the A5 to return to your car.

WALK 10

Cwm Bochlwyd and
Glyder Fach

Start/Finish	Ogwen Cottage car park SH 648 604
Distance	8km (5 miles): an extra 2km (1¼ miles) if the Miners' Track is taken to avoid Bristly Ridge
Total ascent	850m (2790ft)
Grade	Strenuous with some scrambling
Time	5hr
Terrain	Rough paths and, if Bristly Ridge is included, a Grade 1 scramble
Map	OS OL17 Snowdon/Yr Wyddfa
Access	Ogwen Cottage stands at the eastern end of Llyn Ogwen on the A5 about 4 miles south of Bethesda
Parking	There is a pay and display car park by the information centre or free places – although they fill up early – further up the road
Note	Bristly Ridge is a strong contender for the title of the finest Grade 1 scramble in North Wales, and for those who enjoy moving up steep rock on big holds it is an exhilarating route to the top of Glyder Fach. It does, however, include exposed moves and, although the way is now marked by the passing of countless boots and crampons, route finding also requires a little care.

The Nant Ffrancon is so lavishly supplied with opportunities for adventure that first-time visitors, like children in a sweetshop, scarcely know which to snatch up first. Magnificent mountains rear up on both sides of the valley, with naked rock in abundance and all demanding attention. The temptation to wolf it all down at once is almost irresistible. To make this a full horseshoe of Cwm Bochlwyd it ought really to include Tryfan too, but this route leaves that delight for another day. For those determined to gorge on all Ogwen's treats at a single sitting the walk can be combined with the scramble up the Tryfan's North Ridge described in Walk 8, joining the route at Bwlch Tryfan.

Take the pitched path to the left of the information centre, aiming for the rocky west face of Tryfan with the col of Bwlch Tryfan, the day's first objective, clearly in view. After a few minutes the path forks with the main broad track curving off rightwards to Cwm Idwal. ◄ For now take the narrower but still clear path leftwards heading towards Bwlch Tryfan. It continues climbing beside a stream, for most of the way on its right bank, beside a series of attractive waterfalls before eventually crossing on boulders to arrive at the delightfully set **Llyn Bochlwyd**. The path carries on above the right hand shoreline to **Bwlch Tryfan**, which is marked by a ladder stile over the wall: here a decision has to be made

This will be visited later in the day.

map at 1:25,000 scale

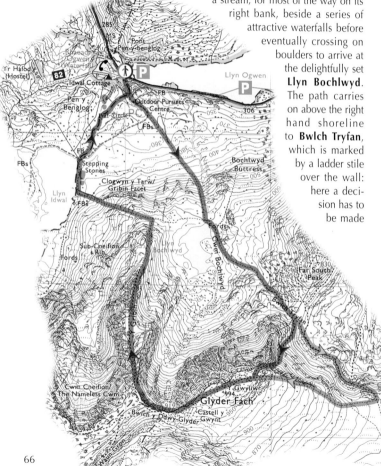

Poised (or is it posed?) on the Cantilever Stone

whether to follow the main route along Bristly Ridge or to avoid the scramble by taking an alternative route along the Miners' Track.

Bristly Ridge rises challengingly to the right and is reached by a vague, loose path up the scree on the right of the wall. Where it reaches the first crags it veers slightly to the right to enter a gully a few metres from the wall. This is climbed past an incongruous section of drystone wall to enter a higher gully before moving out leftwards after which route finding problems ease for a while. The ridge continues until it merges into the hillside at a junction of paths.

Alternative route via Miners' Track (shown in blue)
Those who prefer to avoid the scramble can instead cross the stile and continue along the ascent track, known as the Miners' Track, which was once used by men from Bethesda to reach the workings on Snowdon. This loses a little height, dropping slightly into Cwm Tryfan before climbing again to reach the shoulder of Glyder Fach to join the path coming from Capel Curig. Turn right up this to reach the upper slopes of Glyder Fach and the junction with the top of the path from Bristly Ridge.

The paths converge close to the Cantilever Stone.

The **Cantilever Stone** is a great horizontal slab balanced like a diving board, which must be one of the most photographed bits of rock in Snowdonia.

On sunny days you may have to wait your turn to pose on its tip.

Having taken the obligatory photograph, carry on up the slope to the great pile of jumbled boulders which provides a massive natural cairn – perhaps one piled up by a team of particularly muscular and enthusiastic giants – at the 994m (3261ft) summit of **Glyder Fach**.

From the summit the next landmark is the **Castell y Gwynt** ('Castle of the Winds'), a dramatic collection of shattered pinnacles and spiky standing stones. ◄ Either scramble through ramparts just to the left of the highest rocks or else drop down further left to a path which skirts below it. Beyond the Castell the main path heads off diagonally leftwards, making for the marginally higher summit of Glyder Fawr. Ignore this and instead continue up around the rim of the cwm, aiming for a sharp promontory above **Y Gribin**.

On a misty day, when the cloud boils up out of the cwm below and wisps play among the rocks, the Castell y Gwynt does indeed loom out of the vapour like a sinister fantasy fortress.

Just beyond the top of the spur, which is marked by a circular windbreak, another large cairn signals the start of the descent path, which is initially very eroded as it drops to the left of the narrow crest. ◄ Finally the path reaches a grassy shoulder where the going becomes much easier and there is finally an opportunity to admire the rocky landscape of Cwm Idwal to the left below. As the path descends a pitched section just before reaching **Llyn Bochlwyd** look out for a narrower trod breaking off horizontally leftwards across the hillside. Follow this and within a few minutes reach the rim of Cwm Idwal.

Care is needed on the loose scree of this upper section as it weaves down through rocks.

Cwm Idwal's rock-girt hollow is home to some of the most famous easy climbs in Britain, especially on the vast sweep of boilerplate slabs. It is worth making a diversion into the cwm to admire the huge scale of the rock architecture in this magnificent cirque of rock.

At the shore of **Llyn Idwal** turn right along the broad path and follow it back to the information centre.

WALK 11

Y Garn and the Devil's Kitchen

Start/Finish	Ogwen Cottage SH 648 604
Distance	6.5km (4 miles)
Total ascent	641m (2128ft)
Difficulty	Strenuous
Time	4hr
Terrain	Steep rocky paths in ascent and loose scree paths in descent
Map	OS OL17 Snowdon/Yr Wyddfa
Access	On A5 between Capel Curig and Bethesda
Parking	Pay and display at Ogwen Cottage, free places in laybys on A5 by Llyn Ogwen

Llyn Ogwen is surrounded by eye-catchingly rocky mountains but Y Garn more than holds its own in this august company, overshadowed perhaps only by the shapely tower of Tryfan's preposterously photogenic west face at the head of the valley. This walk reaches Y Garn's sharply spiked summit via some of Snowdonia's most impressive rock scenery, climbing up through Cwm Idwal to escape through a gap in the seemingly impregnable cliffs of the Devil's Kitchen.

From the information centre and café at Ogwen Cottage take the pitched path and rocky stairway to the left of the buildings and go through a decorative iron gate. Continue on the main track, ignoring all side paths until it arrives at the beautifully situated waters of **Llyn Idwal** in its stunning rock-encircled cwm, with the pyramid of Y Garn towering above it. At the lake take the path along the left hand shore, aiming for the huge boilerplate slabs at the far end of the lake.

Generations of trembling beginners have had their **first taste of rock climbing** here and the routes,

Climbers on the Idwal Slabs

map at 1:25,000 scale

especially the classic trinity of Faith, Hope and Charity, have become so polished and smooth that

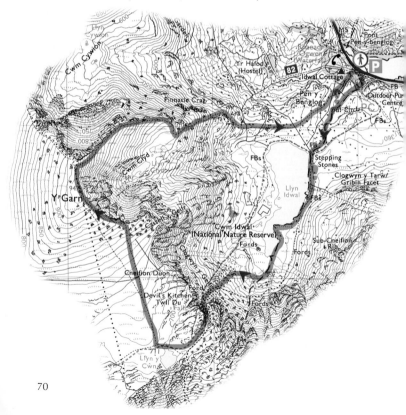

The dark slit of Twll Du and the Devil's Kitchen

experienced climbers will tell you they have become harder and more insecure than many other supposedly far more difficult climbs to be found on less popular cliffs. This, however, seems to have done nothing to dim their popularity and on most days you will probably see climbers on them.

From the slabs carry on up the path as it rises leftwards across the slope, scrambling across a small waterfall on the way and head towards the dark and often dank crags of the **Devil's Kitchen**, split by the dark slash of **Twll Du**, 'The Black Hole'. However, as the foot of the sinister-looking gash in the rocks is neared the engineered path veers away leftwards up the Devil's Staircase to bypass the obstacle. It goes over a stile and then climbs a shallow scree gully to gain the ridge at a col just below the lake of **Llyn y Cwn**.

The path climbing away up the boulders on the left hand slope leads onto Glyder Fawr but our route heads rightwards up the clear path climbing the airy green slope to the pointed 947m (3107ft) summit of **Y Garn**, in marked contrast to the claustrophobic cliffs behind. ◄

This is a perfect lunch spot, often haunted by ravens and seagulls after easy pickings left by walkers on these tops.

> The **views from Y Garn** are stunning, not merely of the long main ridge of the Glyderau stretching away on either hand but also of the huge wall of Pen yr Ole Wen on the other side of the valley, backed by the high tops of the Carneddau beyond. Up the lake is Tryfan, while behind are the pointed summits of the Snowdon Horseshoe.

From the top the disconcertingly steep descent route of the north east ridge is easily picked out. Set off towards the lopsided pyramid of Foel-goch but just after a large cairn the descent path dives down rightwards, with the waters of **Llyn Clyd** and its smaller neighbour clearly visible in the cwm below. The initial steep section is over badly eroded and slippery scree, which demands care before the ridge dwindles to a sharp crest separating **Cwm Clyd** from **Cwm Cywion**. The path clings to the ridge, slithering down another loose section before dropping to **Llyn Idwal**, which in summer is popular with picnicking families and swimmers. ◄ Cross the reservoir's outflow to rejoin the ascent path back to Ogwen Cottage.

With the hard work of the day done it can be very pleasant to wander along the lakeshore before crossing the outflow.

WALK 12
Elidir Fawr and Y Garn

Start/Finish	Nant Peris SH608584
Distance	14km (8½ miles)
Total ascent	1260m (4134ft)
Grade	Strenuous
Time	5hr
Terrain	Good paths
Map	OS OL17 Snowdon/Yr Wyddfa
Access	Nant Peris is on the A4086 in the Llanberis Pass
Parking	Pay and display in Nant Peris

Man has not dealt kindly with Elidir Fawr down the years and there is no disguising the fact. The worst is revealed in the vast terraces of the slate quarries which have been gouged and blasted out of the flank overlooking Llanberis itself. Happily the mountain is big enough to cope and there are other, less ravaged parts to explore, as is proved in this round of four summits including a brace which top the magic 3000ft mark, Elidir Fawr itself at 924m (3031ft) and its even taller neighbour Y Garn at 947m (3107ft).

From the car park turn left towards Llanberis, passing the Vaynol Arms to take a lane on the right by the old chapel and signposted to the campsite. Follow the lane as it swings left past the site entrance and some modern houses, with the vast piles of slate debris filling the view ahead. Where the lane forks by a whitewashed climbing hut go left and after 150 metres or so take the signposted path climbing steeply up the hillside, aiming for the hanging valley of the **Afon Dudodyn** below Elidir Fawr's knobbly ridge.

> The path climbs past **slate tips**, which take on a more mysterious air as the flat-topped stone constructions on their summit give then an air of abandoned Mayan temples. Or is that just imagination trying to undo some of history's harm?

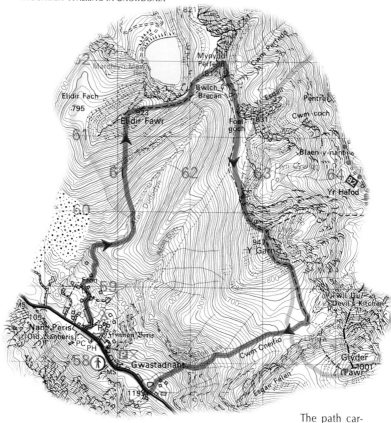

The reservoir is modern man's contribution to the exploitation of the mountain.

The path carries on beside the stream before reaching a flatter section where the route leaves it to cross a footbridge on the left and begin the climb up the grassy spur towards the crest. After a final clamber through a boulder field the path delivers you onto the summit of **Elidir Fawr**, with its circular windbreak. The ridge proves to be sharp and the ground drops away steeply on the other side down to the natural-looking lake of Marchlyn Bach and the decidedly unnatural curving dam of **Marchlyn Mawr**. ◄

Marchlyn Mawr reservoir

Hard as it is to believe, standing on top of Elidir Fawr you are standing on the roof of a power station, **Wales's 'electric mountain'**. The heart of the hill has been hollowed out to create Europe's largest man-made cavern, housing the six huge turbines of the Dinorwig Pump Storage Station. It uses off-peak electricity to lift water from Llyn Peris at the bottom of the mountain up to Marchlyn Mawr. Then, when power is needed, the water is dropped through the turbines to create instant energy. Overall the station actually consumes more power than it produces, but its value is in making use of unwanted electricity to then be able to respond instantly to surges in demand, going from standstill to full output in seconds.

Raising your eyes from the harsh curve of the concrete dam the view is spectacular, out to Anglesey, along the full length of the Carneddau, the Glyderau and Tryfan, round to Snowdon and the southern mountains fading away into mid-Wales.

The path follows the ridge eastwards through the boulders and onto wider grassy slopes before narrowing again to a rocky arête which is descended to Bwlch y Marchlyn. Here the main path heads off rightwards making for the high tops of the Glyderau but carry on straight ahead up the arête and then up a fence line to the grassy top of **Mynydd Perfedd**.

Anyone who thought the name meant **'the perfect mountain'** may be disappointed by the nondescript summit (in fact it means 'middle mountain'), but no one can fail to be impressed by the view, which now includes the folded crags of Pen-yr-Ole-Wen across the Nant Ffrancon and up to the towering east face of Tryfan further up the valley. Closer to hand the green switchback of the ridge to Y Garn draws the eye while, looking back the way we've come, the gable end of Elidir Fawr's summit ridge now appears as a shapely pyramid.

From the summit cross back over the ladder stile used to reach it and then down the grass to **Bwlch y Brecan**. Yet again the main path spurns the climb to the next summit, **Foel-goch**, heading instead directly for Y Garn and it is necessary to leave it to climb the steep zigzags to the summit.

The **top of Foel-goch** is, if anything, even less prepossessing than the summit of Mynydd Perfedd. However it enjoys a main-mast atmosphere, perched on the very rim of the cwm and is the ideal spot to admire the impressive rock architecture of the Glyderau's more rugged side.

By contrast the ridge to Y Garn is broad, green and unmistakeable. At 947m (3107ft) **Y Garn** is the high point of the day in every respect, its sharp rocky summit offering intimate views down into Cwm Idwal and the massive cliffs that loom over it. To descend carry on along the rim of the cwm, aiming for the small lake of **Llyn y Cwn**. At the lake a narrow path breaks off rightwards aiming for a ladder stile on the far side of an uninviting boggy section. Work your way round to the stile as best you can and cross over to follow the improving path down beside the stream. ◄ Where the path comes to a ladder stile leading across the stream ignore it and remain on the same bank all the way down to the road, crossing a small tributary by a footbridge. At the road turn right back into **Nant Peris**.

Along here are some attractive waterfalls.

BETWS-Y-COED

Llyn Crafnant (Walk 13)

WALK 13

Llyn Crafnant and Llyn Geirionydd

Start/Finish	Forestry car park at Llyn Crafnant SH 756 618
Distance	8km (5 miles)
Total ascent	300m (984ft)
Difficulty	Easy
Time	3hr
Terrain	Forest tracks and woodland paths
Map	OS OL17 Snowdon/Yr Wyddfa
Access	The car park is reached by a 2 mile-long single track road from Trefriw on the B5106
Parking	Forestry Commission site near north end of Llyn Crafnant

Much of the walking in Snowdonia is rugged and rocky so this gentle, almost pastoral stroll beside two lakes makes a pleasant contrast and is ideal for a short day or for when the high tops are swathed in cloud. The setting and scale are nigh perfect, and but for a short section after the Taliesin Monument near the end route finding is very simple.

This commemorates the gift of the area to the people of Llanrwst by Richard James in 1896.

From the car park return to the access road and turn right along it. Within a few minutes the road reaches the northern end of **Llyn Crafnant**, the first of the walk's two lakes, and a **monument**. ◄

Just before the monument turn right to cross a bridge over the outflow of the lake and take the forest road running along the northern shore. At a fork take the left hand branch to remain by the water and carry on through several gates, leaving the lake behind, to reach a small cottage called **Hendre**, where the path turns left to cross the valley. It passes a couple of modern houses before reaching a metal gate with a café sign. Go through this and follow the tarmac lane, with exquisite views down the lake and the tree-covered hills on either side.

The farm at Crafnant

After almost a mile and just after passing a house called **Cornel** on the left hand side there is a rather incongruous telephone box. Take a path opposite this which goes through a kissing gate to climb through the trees. After crossing the watershed follow the main forest road as it winds downhill. When it reaches a prominent fork go left following blue waymark signs. At a series of forks keep taking the left

map at 1:25,000 scale

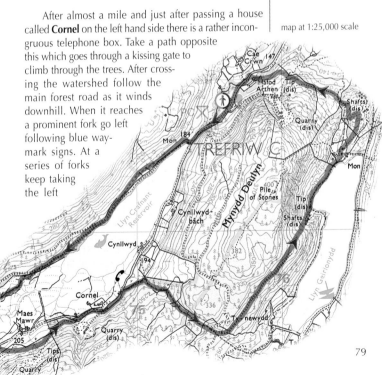

Although the conifers come down to the western shore the view to the east is more open, giving more of mountainous atmosphere than in the adjoining Crafnant Valley.

hand option heading across the slope until the waters of the day's second lake, **Llyn Geirionydd**, come into view just below. ◄ Follow the recently created forestry road and then the more attractive continuation path along the shoreline to the end of the lake, passing an old mine on the way. At the end it meets a farm track with the impressive **Taliesin Monument**, standing on a knoll above the path.

> The **Taliesin Monument** consists of a cross surmounting a standing stone, which itself rests on a plinth of huge blocks. A plaque reveals that it was originally built by Lord Willoughby d'Erisby around 1850 to mark the reputed birthplace of Taliesin, a sixth-century bard who is said to have lived by the lake. The column was destroyed in a storm in 1976 but was rebuilt in 1994 and seems ruggedly appropriate in this wild setting.

From the memorial drop down leftwards to take a narrow grass track marked 'Trefriw Trails 5'. This leads over a low col between the trees and crosses a ladder stile to carry on across the hillside, ignoring the first side path heading uphill. But at the next junction, again marked by a 'Trefriw Trails' sign, take the left hand line which clambers over rock steps and low knolls, at first descending a little but then climbing to cross the shoulder of the ridge to pass more ruined mine buildings. The path crosses a stile and meets a forest road. Take the right hand fork downhill back to the road and car park.

Monument to the bard Taliesin, Llyn Geirionydd

WALK 14

Llyn y Parc and Conwy View

Start/Finish	Betws-y-Coed
Distance	10km (6 miles)
Total ascent	500m (1650ft)
Grade	Moderate
Time	3hr
Terrain	Forest tracks and roads
Map	OS OL17 Snowdon/Yr Wyddfa
Access	Betws-y-Coed is on the A5
Parking	Pont y Pair car park
Notes	Parts of the trail are shared with mountain bikes

Large parts of the Snowdonia National Park are covered with forestry, notably around Coed y Brenin and Beddgelert, as well as by the 7250ha (17,500 acre) Gwydyr Forest around Betws-y-Coed. They are not to everyone's taste but there's no denying they can provide sheltered walking when wild weather makes higher ground unappealing. This walk, setting off from the heart of Betws, climbs to a mountain lake and offers views of the gentle Conwy Valley. It is signposted throughout its length with yellow waymarkers. It must also be said there is a surprising amount of ascent and descent for an outing that never reaches a summit or escapes the trees.

From the Pont y Pair take the side road climbing leftwards up the hill beside the river for about 100 metres and then turn right into a side street marked 'Private road, public footpath', following blue and yellow waymarkers. The tarmac passes between houses before becoming a forestry road. When it reaches a fork by a barrier take the right hand fork and then almost immediately turn up a path to the right. This zigzags steeply uphill through the trees on a carpet of rocks and pine needles. ▶

At the top of the slope the track swings right and passes through an area of younger broadleaf growth

Already the visitor bustle of Betws is far behind and all that can be heard is birdsong.

Map labels: Pont Fawr, P, Gwydir Castle, Gwydir Uchaf Chapel, Mine dis, Berth-ddu, Pen-y-parc, 60, A470, Parc Uchaf Gwydir, Siambar-wen, Drws Gwyn, 59, 11, Afon Conwy, Hafod, Cwmlanerch, 58, Rhyd-y-Creuau, Clogwyn Cyrrau, Coedcynhélier, Miners, Br, MS, CH, Mus, BETWS-Y-COED, P

As with most forest trails, distant views are at a premium so enjoy this one.

before dropping beside old mine workings and joining a forestry road. Turn left along this.

Where the road bends sharply leftwards branch off right into the trees on another waymarked path. When this comes to a forest road turn right and follow it as it traverses round the hillside with glimpses through the trees of the Conwy Valley below. Where it shrinks to become a path carry on and then drop down a flight of rustic steps as it undulates through the trees. Where it meets a road turn right to quickly come to the long finger of **Llyn y Parc**. ◄

Ignore the road cutting back rightwards, signed to Betws, which will be part of the return route. Press on along the forestry road, initially following the lake but then veering away, and turn rightwards to reach a four way junction: here turn right. The track loses height before starting a long traverse around the hillside, with better views across the Conwy Valley and coming to a viewpoint with picnic tables.

This is also the surprising site of an **historic bowling green** laid out 400 years ago by wealthy local landowner Sir John Gwydir to entertain guests on his estate. King Henry VIII had placed a hefty charge on greens, which he feared diverted his subjects from more useful pursuits, so to possess one was quite a status symbol, a message hammered home by the addition of lavish hospitality and entertainment.

Llyn y Parc

From here turn up the left fork of the road, heading back uphill and still following waymarks. At the top of a rise the road comes to a fork, bear right to reach another viewpoint and a rustic sculpture. A few metres further on take a path which climbs leftwards to re-join the road. Turn right along it for a few paces before being directed left again to climb past another sculpture and then on up the hill.

Where it reaches a road turn left up this and go on to a T-junction and turn right still following the waymarkers. At the next fork go left and after 300 metres look for a marked path dropping down to the right with a no cycling sign.

It soon reaches the shore of **Llyn y Parc** and follows the bank all the way to the end of the lake where it returns to the road junction passed on the outward leg. This time take the route straight on, signed to Betws-y-Coed.

The track narrows as it descends, passing a white-washed cottage, and follows a tumbling stream down a steep narrow valley, which forms the prettiest part of the whole walk.

*Pont y Pair Falls in
Betws-y-Coed*

When the track reaches a forest road turn right (downhill) to leave the wood and when it reaches tarmac again turn downhill and carry on down to Pont y Pair.

SNOWDON

The approach to Lliwedd (Walk 17)

WALK 15

Moel Eilio Horseshoe

Start/Finish	Llanberis centre
Distance	14km (9 miles)
Total ascent	990m (3250ft)
Grade	Moderate
Time	4–5hr
Terrain	Grassy tracks. One very steep descent
Map	OS OL17 Snowdon/Yr Wyddfa
Parking	On and off street parking in Llanberis

Thanks to the Snowdon Railway, which sets off from its centre, the name of Llanberis is inextricably linked with Wales's highest summit. But if any mountain can truly claim to belong to the village is it Moel Eilio, rising as it does almost from its main street. However, this horseshoe could scarcely be more different from its better known neighbour, just 3km away as the raven flies but a world away in temperament. Where Snowdon's horseshoe is all jagged rock, narrow crests and high drama Moel Eilio is broad, gentle ridges, mostly friendly angles and springy turf. And it is quiet. When the visitors are queuing for their selfies on Snowdon's overcrowded cairn you might be lucky enough to have this entire circuit to yourself or at least be sharing it with only a handful of discerning fellow walkers.

The long smooth ridge of Moel Eilio

From the main street walk up Ffordd Capel Goch, almost opposite the Padarn Lake Hotel, which was once the focal point of Welsh rock climbing, having been the meeting place and bragging venue for those pushing standards in the 1960s. It was the scene of legendary booze-ups, occasional punch-ups and marathon darts games where information was shared or withheld according to your place in the constantly shifting pecking order.

Carry on past the chapel to Pen-y-Bont and turn right into Fron Goch. At the top of the first steep climb turn left up a lane signposted to Plas Garnedd, heading up towards the rounded top of Moel

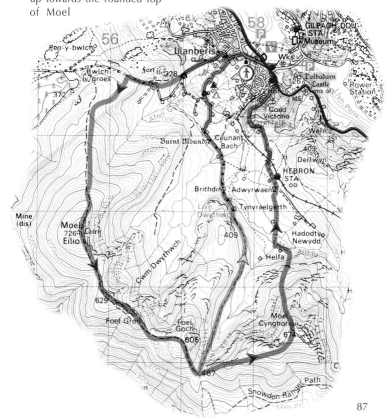

Moel Eilio's vast summit shelter with Snowdon beyond

Eilio. The lane carries on uphill: ignore footpath signs to left and right, continue when the lane becomes a grass track, and reach a gate and ladder stile. Go through this and take the left hand fork as it curves round, aiming for the long, smooth ridge of Moel Eilio. Go through another metal gate and a couple of hundred yards further on look out for a faint grassy vehicle track branching off leftwards. Take this as it climbs up beneath the power lines and follow the improving path for the long easy climb to the summit of **Moel Eilio**.

This is crowned with an impressively tall and well-built **circular wind shelter** but the views in all directions are so superb and far reaching that it would be a shame to sit inside it in all but the foulest weather. The panorama sweeps from the coast past the Carneddau, Glyderau, Tryfan, on over Snowdon to the ridges of the south, including the impressive Nantlle. In between the rest of the horseshoe stretches away in a beckoning green switchback towards Snowdon's distant pointed summit.

The descent follows an old fence line heading south east around the rim of the cwm dropping down soft turf with Llyn Dwythwch below. The summits of **Foel Gron** and **Foel Goch** pass almost unnoticed, their rounded tops unadorned by cairns or wind shelters. ▸

From the top of Foel Goch drop down steeply to the col of Bwlch Maesgwm.

Alternative return to Llanberis

This is a high mountain pass crossed by a wide and well-made path which provides a useful escape route in bad weather as well as a temptingly quick return to Llanberis and, it must be said, a much easier one than is to be found down the untracked slopes from the final summit, Moel Cynghorion, which stretches away above.

However, to complete the horseshoe cross the ladder stile and follow the ridge upwards.

After a long green climb the path arrives on the summit of **Moel Cynghorion**, a large grassy field almost as unadorned as its predecessors but for a ladder stile, a puddle-sized tarn and a cairn so small it is more of a trip hazard than a landmark. ▸

Go over the ladder stile, taking a lingering look across at Snowdon and below it the huge face of Clogwyn du'r Arddu.

The **'Black Cliff'**, perhaps the most fearsome expanse of rock in Britain, is where the legendary climber Joe Brown, who went on to make his home in Llanberis, first carved out his reputation in the 1950s. Even today 'Cloggy' is still spoken of in awed tones.

Head northwards making for the distant rooftops of Llanberis. The ridge is pathless and initially a very steep grassy slope. The going is fairly straightforward, aiming for a track heading across the valley below, but hard work on the knees. Eventually the ridge arrives behind a restored bunkhouse with a ladder stile beside it. ▸

From the bunkhouse take the access track and follow it to a lane arriving close to **Hebron Station** on the Snowdon Railway. Turn left down the tarmac and follow the lane down to the edge of the village.

It's almost as if the horseshoe has decided it has done enough with the exuberant construction on top of Moel Eilio.

The name means 'Hill of the Counsellors', but I'd be wary of taking advice from any group which chose such a forlorn spot for their deliberations

Do not be tempted to aim for the gate to the left as it is defended by a quagmire moat.

WALK 16
Snowdon Horseshoe

Start/Finish	Pen-y-Pass car park at the top of the Llanberis Pass SH 648 557
Distance	11km (7 miles)
Total ascent	1100m (3575ft)
Grade	Strenuous with exposed scrambling
Time	6–7hr
Terrain	Narrow, exposed ridges and steep, sometimes eroded, paths
Map	OS OL17 Snowdon/Yr Wyddfa
Parking	Pen-y-Pass has a large car park but even at an exorbitant £10 per day it can fill up very early at peak periods. Alternatively there is a youth hostel or it can be reached by a bus service from Llanberis or Nant Peris.
Note	Although one of the finest and most popular walks and scrambles in the country for those with a head for heights the Snowdon Horseshoe should not be underestimated. In fine weather it makes a magnificent day out but the exposed ridges are best avoided in windy or wet weather and under winter conditions can become positively Alpine, demanding full winter climbing equipment.

Mention that you have been walking in North Wales and someone will almost inevitably ask if you did 'The Horseshoe', and despite all the alternatives there is no doubting which one they mean. The Snowdon Horseshoe is *the* walk, taking in some of the most spectacular summits, airy ridges and jaw-dropping mountain scenery with a grandeur that even a mountaintop café and tourist railway cannot entirely undermine.

The route starts up **the PyG Track**, whose name remains a source of contention. Some say it takes its name from the Pen y Gwryd hotel further down the A4086 while others contend it is from Bwlch y Moch, 'the pass of the pigs', further up the slope.

Whichever explanation you prefer, the track leaves the top right hand corner of the car park aiming for the shapely cone of Crib Goch, the first objective of the day. On this section you will probably be following crowds making for Snowdon's summit. After about ¾hr of almost unremitting ascent you are rewarded with the appearance of **Llyn Llydaw** cradled in its cwm, with the pointed summit of Snowdon itself towering above. The main path carries on straight ahead to reach the lake but a narrower, more enticing track heads up rightwards towards the beckoning summit of **Crib Goch**. ▶

After about a third of the ascent the route becomes a full-blooded scramble, taking in short walls and polished slabs and the hands will be in almost constant use until the slopes of Garnedd Ugain are reached. Although the climb demands a modicum of agility and a head for heights the scrambling is never desperate and it is usually possible to find an easier way round the major difficulties.

From the top – following a well-deserved rest – the ridge stretches away in a curving tightrope of ruddy rock to the three towers at the far end and then over the continuation ridges of Crib Y Ddysgl and Garnedd Ugain before Snowdon itself. ▶

The crossing of Crib Goch ends with clambering over the final towers, which appear daunting but prove quite straightforward once you get to grips with them. Beyond

A warning sign on a stile announcing this as the route to Crib Goch only adds to the frisson of excitement.

Whatever other difficulties the ridge may hold navigation is seldom one of them, the way polished by myriad boots and scarred by the points of countless crampons.

Crib Goch Pinnacles

the path rises in a series of scrambles of **Crib y Ddysgl** to the trig point on **Garnedd Ugain**. From here the character of the walk changes almost beyond recognition as you join the crowds who have come either up the gentler PyG Track or trudged the even more placid tourist path from Llanberis. The summit railway also makes its appearance, with the final stretch of track sharing the summit ridge with the often congested path.

Victorian can-do engineering marvel or environmental abomination, there are few who don't have an opinion on the **summit railway** and the café it spawned. Since it opened in 1896, in the face of determined opposition from the then newly formed National Trust, the railway has taken millions of

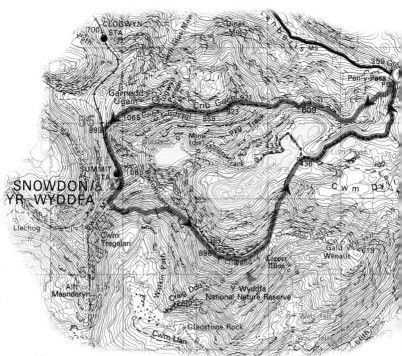

people to the 1085m (3560ft) peak. The line, created purely for tourism, made use of rack and pinion technology developed in the Alps and climbs gradients as steep as 1:7 along its 8km (5 mile) route. At the top passengers find the Hafod Eryri, a café and visitor centre rebuilt in 2009 which manages to exude all the mountain charm of a motorway services and has persuaded many a sensitive mountain lover to forswear a visit to the roof of Wales ever again.

From the summit the continuation ridge to Y Lliwedd is obvious, but the direct route drops down hideously eroded scree. It is better to avoid most of this by following signs for the Watkin Path, which drops past the entrance to the café. After a couple of hundred metres, at a tall and unmistakeable marker stone, the path curls back towards Y Lliwedd, but even this route does not avoid all the erosion problems and eventually it too deteriorates into countless variations through the wilderness of scree. The easiest route sticks well to the right (facing outwards) but none is without its

*First objective:
Crib Goch*

93

discomforts and suffice to say that whichever you choose you will probably wish you had picked another.

Doubtless **path repairs** are on someone's To Do list and the sooner the better. Until then this once-delightful track will always be a less-than-enticing way to and from the summit.

This provides numerous pleasant scrambling options, although none as exciting as Crib Goch.

When it reaches the col of Bwlch Ciliau, below **Y Lliwedd**, the Watkin Path turns sharply rightwards towards the valley. Ignore this and instead carry on up the rocky tower ahead. ◄

From the path there are views of the extensive but now unfashionable **North Face of Y Lliwedd**. This huge sweep of cliff was popular with the early pioneer climbers but was later eclipsed by steeper fare such as Clogwyn du'r Arddu on the opposite side of the mountain, the Three Cliffs of the Llanberis Pass and, more recently the sea cliffs of Craig Gogarth on Anglesey. Perhaps as unclimbed rock becomes at a premium the crag may return to vogue.

Carry on over the two rocky tops and then follow the path down and round the ridge, making for **Llyn Llydaw** below. At the water's edge turn right and join the broad and well surfaced Miners' Track back to **Pen-y-Pass**.

WALK 17

Snowdon via Miners' Track and PyG Track

Start/Finish	Pen-y-Pass car park at the top of the Llanberis Pass SH 648 557
Distance	11km (7 miles)
Total ascent	750m (2461ft)
Difficulty	Moderate
Time	5–6hr
Terrain	Good paths
Map	OS OL17 Snowdon/Yr Wyddfa
Access	Pen-y-Pass on the A4086 at the top of the Llanberis Pass
Parking	Pen-y-Pass has a large car park but even at an exorbitant £10 per day it can fill up very early at peak periods. Alternatively there is a youth hostel or it can be reached by a bus service from Llanberis or Nant Peris.

Snowdon is buttressed by airy rocky ridges that will set any seasoned scrambler's pulse racing, but for those who prefer to avoid the rigours of Crib Goch and to spare themselves the long trudge from Llanberis while still enjoying dramatic mountain scenery there are two paths which together offer an easier solution, albeit at the expense of covering a little of the same ground twice. The Miners' Track and the PyG Track both begin from the pay and display car park at Pen-y-Pass at the top of the Llanberis Pass. The walk could as easily be done in either direction, but climbing the Miners' Track has two distinct advantages. Firstly it offers a gentler introduction to warm up the legs for the effort to come and, perhaps more importantly, attracts fewer people early in the day.

Leave the car park via a marked gate in the top left hand corner.

> This is the start of the **Miners' Track**, built to serve the now long-defunct Britannia Copper Mine. Although the mine is now just ruins the track is kept

in good condition as it still serves the water station at Llyn Llydaw, which in turn feeds the very visible pipeline dropping down to the hydroelectric station in Cwm Dyli below.

As the path breasts a rise the whole of the Snowdon Horseshoe, from Lliwedd, past the pointed pyramid of Snowdon itself and round to Garnedd Ugain and Crib Goch, leaps into view with the path stretching away ahead into the very heart of the mountains and promising great things to come. The track passes a smaller lake, **Llyn Teyrn**, with the old miners' barracks whose roofless ruins reveal a line of tiny, cell-like rooms.

After a gentle half hour the path reaches **Llyn Llydaw**, cupped in the bed of the cwm. Ignore the side track leading off towards the ugly building of the water station and instead carry on along the main path to cross a causeway and follow it along the opposite shore.

The PyG Track crosses the slopes above and the voices of walkers using it will often be heard.

From the lake the path turns steeply upwards, following a recently repitched section, quickly gaining height until it arrives at the smaller sheet of **Glaslyn**, its waters tinged green by copper deposits. ◄ Circle Glaslyn as far as the ruined mine buildings.

Copper was mined on these slopes for more than a century by a string of companies, none of

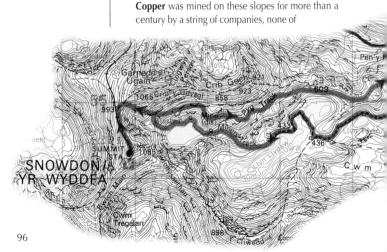

The ruins of the Britannia mine

which proved particularly successful, and the mine finally closed in 1916 when even the demands of the war effort could not save it. Today all that is left is a collection of roofless buildings open to the sky, odd scraps of machinery and the colourful debris of the spoil heaps.

From the mine buildings climb the stepped path heading up through the scree and boulders to a junction with the PyG Track, marked by a slender carved standing stone. Here turn left, with the way no longer in any doubt. From now on the route will also get busier. As the route nears the col you will be joined by those hardly pilgrims who have made their way over Crib Goch, and shortly afterwards by those who have made the longer, if less steep, trek from Llanberis. ▶ Once the 1085m (3560ft) summit of **Snowdon** is reached train passengers will add to the throng queuing to stand on the roof of Wales.

Take careful note of this junction as you will not want to miss it on the way back down.

It is sometimes cynically said that the **summit railway** and new café are allowed to exist solely as a warning to ensure that nothing similar is ever allowed to happen again. Yet for all its drawbacks the summit remains a magnificent viewpoint, with the whole of Snowdonia laid before you, views stretching away to the coast and eastwards back to England.

It might also be argued that this is the most democratic summit in the whole land, not reserved solely for climbers and walkers but available to all-comers, thanks to the railway which ferries everyone from babes in arms to venerable grandmothers in flimsy sandals to the summit to enjoy the view and to sit awhile in the café before being gently transported back to civilisation.

To return to Pen-y-Pass, retrace your steps down the final ridge paralleling the railway line to the col at the head of the PyG Track noted on the ascent and then turn back down the way you came up as far as the standing stone marking the junction with the Miners' Track above Glaslyn, but this time carry on straight ahead, following the clear **PyG Track** over the col at Bwlch y Moch. Here take a last look back at Snowdon's shapely summit pyramid towering over Llyn Llydaw before carrying on down the steeply stepped path back to **Pen-y-Pass**, the car park and another couple of cafés.

The busy PyG Track, one of the most popular ways up and down Snowdon

WALK 18

Lliwedd via the Miners' Track and Y Gribin

Start/Finish	Pen-y-Pass car park at the top of the Llanberis Pass SH 648 557
Distance	11km (7 miles)
Total ascent	539m (1768ft)
Difficulty	Strenuous with a scramble
Time	4–5hr
Terrain	Good paths followed by a Grade 1 scramble: head for heights required
Parking	Pen-y-Pass has a large car park but even at an exorbitant £10 per day it can fill up very early at peak periods. Alternatively there is a youth hostel or it can be reached by a bus service from Llanberis or Nant Peris.
Notes	Although much less well-known and shorter than its celebrated neighbour, Crib Goch, the ridge of Y Gribin is probably of similar difficulty and should not be underestimated. Relatively straightforward in good conditions, it is best avoided in high winds or wet weather and under winter conditions becomes a full-blown climb demanding ice axes, crampons and even ropes.

In any other company Lliwedd would be an irresistible peak, rising hundreds of feet up steep cliffs to a double summit from the banks of Llyn Llydaw cupped in its glacial cwm. As it is, flanked by the towering bulk of Snowdon and staring across the void to the tightrope ridge of Crib Goch, Lliwedd is often unjustly relegated to a bit part player at the end of the day, almost an afterthought on the circuit of the superb Snowdon Horseshoe. It deserves far better.

This route elevates this pointed, rocky summit to centre stage and has the added bonus of including a fine scramble which you are quite likely to have to yourself even on days when its more famous companions are under siege from an endless stream of suitors. It also allows Lliwedd to be enjoyed without having to visit the top of Snowdon, which many purists find depressingly defiled with its café and railway station.

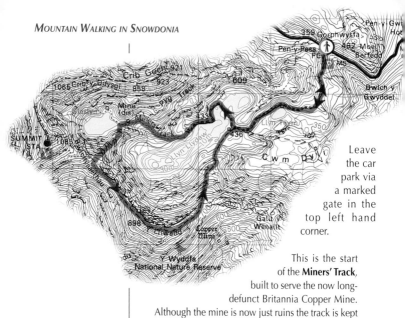

Leave the car park via a marked gate in the top left hand corner.

This is the start of the **Miners' Track**, built to serve the now long-defunct Britannia Copper Mine. Although the mine is now just ruins the track is kept in good condition as it still serves the water station at Llyn Llydaw, which in turn feeds the very visible pipeline dropping down to the hydroelectric station in Cwm Dyli below.

Lliwedd and Y Gribin from Glaslyn

As the path breasts a rise the whole of the Snowdon Horseshoe, from Lliwedd, past the pointed pyramid of Snowdon itself and round to Garnedd Ugain and Crib Goch, leaps into view with the path stretching away ahead into the very heart of the mountains and promising great things to come. The track passes a smaller lake, **Llyn Teyrn**. ▶

After a gentle half hour the path reaches **Llyn Llydaw**, cupped in the bed of the cwm. Ignore the side track leading off towards the ugly building of the water station and instead carry on along the main path to cross a causeway and follow it along the opposite shore.

From the lake the path turns steeply upwards, following a recently repitched section, quickly gaining height until it arrives at the smaller sheet of **Glaslyn**, its waters tinged green by copper deposits. Cross the outlet of the lake on stepping stones and then follow the narrow grassy trod up the hillside opposite. The narrowness of the path, a marked contrast from the engineered steps of the Miners' Track, shows just how few walk Y Gribin compared with the more popular routes up Snowdon, which have either been engineered like the PyG and the Miners' Tracks, or trampled into eroded scree like the Watkin's upper reaches.

Here is an old miners' barracks whose roofless ruins reveal a line of tiny, cell-like rooms.

The start of the scrambling on Y Gribin

The track initially makes a rising traverse up the side of the ridge to reach the crest, with Glaslyn to one side and **Llyn Llydaw** on the other. Above this col the ridge rises in a series of short slabs and ribs. The easiest way tends to be on the left hand side but competent scramblers will be able to pick their way up the ridge almost anywhere with no shortage of options to revel in the magnificent situations and solitude. The scrambling ends all too soon at a large cairn in an eagle's nest position overlooking Glaslyn, with the pyramid of Snowdon above to the right while to the left are the alluring pointed tops of Y Lliwedd itself, perched above the vast slabs of its own north face. This grassy belvedere also makes an excellent refreshment stop for those who prefer mountain solitude to crowded summits. ◄

You may have parties of climbers to entertain you while you regain your breath, but Lliwedd is a much less fashionable crag these days than once it was.

From the cairn carry on up the slope ahead to reach the rim of the cwm and then follow the intermittent path leftwards towards Y Lliwedd. The path occasionally strays very close to the edge and in poor visibility it may be better to continue over the back of the cwm and drop a short way down the south western slope to join the Watkin Path descending from Snowdon (Walk 16). Whichever route is chosen, carry on until the path reaches Bwlch Ciliau, the col below **Y Lliwedd**, where the Watkin Path takes a sharp right turn downhill into Cwm Llan, and then scramble up the broken path and rocks to the summit with its superb views across to Snowdon and the surrounding tops. This section can be made almost as easy or as hard as you please: a relatively straightforward path snakes its way up between the rocks or, if you prefer a little more scrambling, pick your way up the mini-crags and ridges. ◄

Be careful not to stray onto the huge face of Y Lliwedd's vast northern frontage.

Carry on over the two rocky tops and then follow the path down and round the ridge, making for **Llyn Llydaw** below. At the water's edge turn right and join the broad and well surfaced Miners' Track back to **Pen-y-Pass**.

WALK 19

Snowdon via the Watkin and
Rhyd Ddu Paths

Start/Finish	Pay and display car park at Pont Bethania SH 628 507
Distance	12.5km (8 miles)
Total ascent	1050m (3445ft)
Grade	Strenuous
Time	6hr
Terrain	Good tracks
Map	OS OL17 Snowdon/Yr Wyddfa
Access	On the A498 at Nantgwynant between Pen y Gwryd and Beddgelert
Parking	Pay and display car park at Nant Gwynant or possibility of free parking in the layby just beyond the café towards Beddgelert

Many would say that the Watkin Path is actually the most arduous way up Snowdon. It may lack the technical difficulties of the scramble over Crib Goch but it combines a long approach and steep gradients with the lowest start of all the major routes up Wales's highest peak. Every vertical metre must be earned, unlike the popular routes from Pen-y-Pass, which begin almost 300m (980ft) higher. It all adds up to a tough day out but in return it offers the reward of an attractive walk up Cwm Llan, with an unusual perspective on Lliwedd and the sudden revelation of the peaks of the Snowdon Horseshoe in its upper reaches. It will also be far quieter than the paths from Pen-y-Pass or Llanberis.

The path, named after a Victorian railway owner, Sir Edward Watkin, who had it built, begins innocuously enough. Cross the road from the car park and turn towards Beddgelert. Within a few metres the signed path starts at a flight of stone steps before entering delightful woodland of moss-encrusted oaks filled with the sound of birds and running water. The path emerges from the

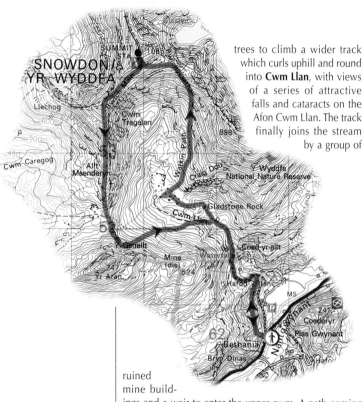

trees to climb a wider track which curls uphill and round into **Cwm Llan**, with views of a series of attractive falls and cataracts on the Afon Cwm Llan. The track finally joins the stream by a group of ruined mine buildings and a weir to enter the upper cwm. A path coming down from the left is our return route: ignore it for now and stay on the broad track which crosses the river on a bridge for a welcome flatter section after the long initial climb.

The path continues into the upper cwm to reach yet more ruined buildings and a heap of slate spoil, where it begins the long climb to Bwlch Ciliau between Y Lliwedd and Snowdon. Behind, the perfect cone of Yr Aran rises on the opposite side of the valley. The track, although designed as a path up Snowdon, seems determined to attack **Y Lliwedd** instead and arrives at a sprawling cairn at the foot of that peak's north east ridge, should you wish to add an extra top to the day.

Approaching the infamous zigzags to Snowdon's summit. It's best to keep left

The main path turns sharp left, traversing just below the crest of the ridge and aiming for the shattered front of Snowdon's final pyramid. As it approaches the final climb the path moves closer to the crest of the ridge. ▶

This final slope is a minor annexe of Purgatory. The hitherto clear path degenerates into a maze of minor trods, each searching for its own way through the scree. None of the options seems to be the right one but some are definitely more wrong than others. The slope around you is likely to be dotted with walkers going both up and down and all looking vainly for a better choice than the one they are on. The best routes are to the left hand edge of the screes.

All bad things eventually come to an end and at the top of the slope is a standing stone marking the junction with the Rhyd Ddu Path. Turn right up the ridge and within a few minutes the café and then the 1085m (3560ft) summit of **Snowdon** are reached.

The **views from Snowdon**, as might be expected from the highest peak in Wales, are superb in all directions but the peaks of the Snowdon Horseshoe,

Here are views across to Crib Goch and down to the ore-stained screes of Glaslyn below.

105

and especially the ridge of Crib Goch across the valley steal the show. Beyond rise the rocky tops of the Glyderau.

From the summit retrace your steps back past the café and down to the standing stone at the junction of the Watkin and Rhyd Ddu Paths, but this time follow the Rhyd Ddu signs heading straight down the ridge. Within a couple of hundred metres from the summit it is not unusual to find you have the ridge to yourself, the bulk of the crowds which thronged the summit having dispersed to the train, the tourist path from Llanberis or down the Watkin, heading for Lliwedd and the final peak of the Horseshoe.

Snowdon's south ridge deserves far more attention than it gets. In any other company it would be considered a 'must-do' walk, poised above the void of Cwm Llan to the east and the scattering of lakes, notably Llyn Cwellyn, to the west, with the shining sea beyond: but it cannot compete with Crib Goch and Y Lliwedd.

The ridge continues dropping gently, with a brief rocky interlude to cross the minor top of **Allt Maenderyn**, to reach Bwlch Cwm Llan below the emphatic arête of **Yr Aran**. ◄ Turn left downhill taking one of the several paths which eventually join in the upper cwm to descend rather soggily to a well-made mine track which traverses easily rightwards across the slope. After a few minutes a pitched path breaks off downhill. Follow this down to the main Watkin Path to join it by the weir passed on the ascent. Turn right and retrace the outward route back to the car park at the end of a long but satisfying day.

If energy and daylight permit it is possible to carry on over this peak using the description in Walk 20, but it is a daunting prospect at the end of what is already a long day.

WALK 20

Yr Aran

Start/Finish	Pay and display car park at Pont Bethania SH 628 507
Distance	10km (6 miles)
Total ascent	805m (2640ft)
Grade	Moderate
Time	4hr
Terrain	Hill tracks wet in places
Map	OS OL17 Snowdon/Yr Wyddfa
Access	On the A498 at Nant Gwynant between Pen y Gwryd and Beddgelert
Parking	Pay and display car park at Pont Bethania or possibility of free parking in the layby just beyond the café towards Beddgelert

There are many reasons for climbing a mountain. Some demand attention for their height, others for their fame and a select few because they're just so beautiful they are impossible to ignore. Yr Aran is one of the latter, a pin-up peak which flaunts itself on calendars and postcards. Its perfect pyramid sits at the end of Llyn Gwynant, beckoning you on. Although officially part of the Snowdon massif, at 747m (2451ft) it is a relative tiddler compared to its loftier siblings, and its position, aloof from the rest of the family, means that it is seldom included in most walkers' visits to the main group. They have bigger and more dramatic fish to fry. If you meet another walker on Yr Aran is it because they have been seduced by its perfect shape: they want to be there.

From the car park cross the road and within a few paces take the Watkin Path up a flight of stone steps. ▶ When the path leaves the trees it joins a stony track which curls up through lower **Cwm Llan**, beside a series of waterfalls and cataracts coming down from Snowdon and passing a steep engineered incline, a remnant from the days of mining and quarrying on the mountain.

This first section is through a mixed woodland of oak, beech and birch and it is hard to imagine a more pleasant start to any walk.

When it reaches the top of a slope by a small weir it is time to leave the Watkin Path for a pitched track on the left which rises towards Bwlch Cwm Llan. Within a hundred metres or so it meets a miners' track crossing the slope. Turn right along this. After about 500 level metres, and where the track cuts through a rocky spur, take a grassy track climbing leftwards through the grass and rushes towards the col.

Here, after crossing a band of scree and climbing a short gully, the path meets a drystone wall. Turn left beside it and drop down a few metres to cross the col to climb the ridge of **Yr Aran** beside the wall. Where the wall turns sharply left follow it as it crosses the slopes with the screes and minor crags of Yr Aran's north face above.

The path continues its steadily rising traverse to arrive on the easier angled East Ridge. ◄ Follow the clear path by a line of old iron fence posts onto the summit cairn, which is perched directly above the north face just crossed.

Note this junction as it is needed on the descent.

Thanks to its semi-detached position from the main Snowdon massif, **Yr Aran's summit** is a perfect viewpoint not just for Snowdon and Y Lliwedd but the surrounding peaks and away to the south and west. It also has a satisfyingly isolated feeling, perched on the very nosecone of the hill.

The descent begins by retracing your footsteps down the line of old fence posts but at the junction met on the way up carry on straight ahead down the ridge with a drystone wall for company. Where the wall turns away rightwards carry on straight ahead following the grassy trod down the broad ridge, initially aiming for the waters of Llyn Gwynant in the valley below and the peak of Moel Siabod beyond. However, before long the increasingly vague trod starts to move leftwards taking you back down into the valley of **Cwm Llan**, which you ascended on the Watkin Path.

Soon the network of miners' tracks used on the ascent comes into view. Aim for these and use them to

Yr Aran from Llyn Gwynant

map at 1:25,000 scale

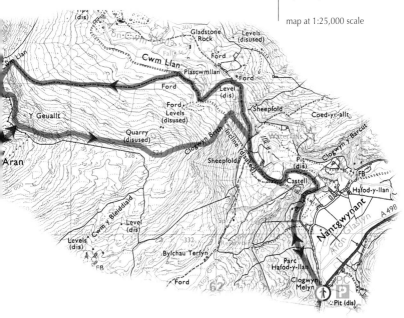

The Watkin Path through the initial woods

regain the Watkin Path to return to the car park. If on reaching the horizontal track used on the ascent you are tempted to follow it rightwards to avoid retracing your steps be aware that it leads to the top of the engineered incline seen on the way up. While this is a feasible, if disconcertingly steep, line of descent it is a much less comfortable route than the main path and, unless you are unlucky, a much slower one too.

EIFIONYDD

Starting the climb to Y Garn (Walk 23)

WALK 21

*Cwm Pennant and the
Moel Hebog ridge*

Start/Finish	Cwmystradllyn SH 557 442
Distance	15km (9½ miles)
Total ascent	750m (2460ft)
Grade	Strenuous
Time	6hr
Terrain	Long valley, wet and trackless in places, and a high ridge; pathless sections
Maps	OS OL17 Snowdon/Yr Wyddfa and OS OL18 Harlech, Porthmadog and Y Bala
Access	From the roundabout at the western end of Tremadog take the A487 towards Caernarfon and after 1½ miles turn right along a narrow road signed to Golan and Cwmystradllyn. After another ¾ mile turn right onto a narrower lane signed to Cwmystradllyn. Where the road appears to end at a house turn right to reach the tiny car park by the dam.
Parking	Picnic area by the dam of Llyn Cwmystradllyn

Moel Hebog, the emphatic exclamation mark at the end of a long rocky ridge, towers over Beddgelert, throwing down a clear challenge to walkers lolling in the cafés and pubs. But an ascent from that side means a long, claustrophobic trudge up through the conifers of Beddgelert Forest. There is another way to this attractive summit via the long and lonely valley of Cwm Pennant, which makes the perfect antidote to the crowded tops of nearby Snowdon and the Glyderau.

From the car park walk back up the road to the junction by a house at **Tyddyn Mawr** and turn left back down the road and follow it for a few minutes to the right hand bend by the access track to **Traian**. Go up the track and at a fork by the farm go right through a gate, passing above

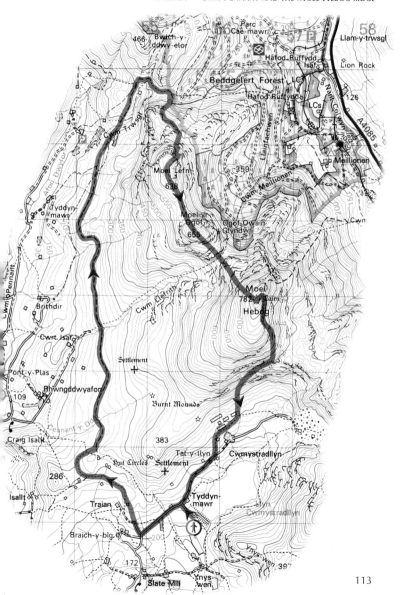

the farm buildings to begin the long ascent of Cwm Pennant, following an old slate tramway that leads all the way to the head of the valley.

The hills are slowly reclaiming the track, which is not always easy to follow. Sometimes it is clear but at others it vanishes completely and you are guided only by the tops of ladder stiles peeping above the rushes. Pondering which way you would take if you had the misfortune to have to navigate slate tubs across such uncooperative terrain is sometimes the easiest way to follow its line.

Away to the left the sea lends an extra dimension to the walk and helps to dispel some of the melancholy that seems to linger in this **deserted and often neglected landscape**, which is dotted with roofless buildings. They bear silent witness to earlier times when the valley was much more populated, in the days before the slate industry died and farming families gave up the unequal struggle against the thin soil. It is a world away for the crowds who jostle for the summit of Snowdon or even the pavements of Beddgelert.

The decaying tramway through Cwn Pennant

Ahead the scalloped line of the Nantlle Ridge maintains interest, lifts the spirits and draws you on. The path crosses several dilapidated and disintegrating bridges before reaching a deep gorge where the stone span has been dismantled. However, a few steps upstream reveal a wooden replacement, and the track carries on up the valley. As the tramway worms deeper into the hills it becomes even harder to follow – it often veers further left than expected – but eventually it or one of the umpteen variations it has spawned across the skirts of Moel Lefn will deliver you to the derelict buildings of the former Prince of Wales quarry.

Climb up towards the terraces of slate spoil beneath the seemingly impenetrable crags on the flank of the mountain. The path traverses above a dam and climbs to the upper levels of spoil where a path crosses the terrace to a clear track climbing up through the boulders and heather to the ridge.

The crest provides a surprise when, after the vast spaces of Cwm Pennant, you find yourself brushing against the serried Christmas trees of **Beddgelert Forest**. Ignore all paths heading into the trees and instead climb beside the wall skirting the plantations, passing a mining tunnel on the way, and aiming for the now hidden top of **Moel Lefn**. At the top of the wall the path shrugs off the trees to give panoramic views to the south and east as it zigzags up a broad open shoulder to arrive on the 638m (2094ft) summit plateau, which is crowned by a rocky tor.

> The **views from Moel Lefn** are simply breathtaking, looking across the vast chasm of Cwm Pennant to Craig Cwm Silyn and the rest of the Nantlle Ridge, round to Snowdon, the shapely pyramid of Cnicht and the Moelwyns and down the coast. Small wonder that Eifion Wyn, the shepherd poet, was moved to write: 'Oh God, why didst Thou make Cwm Pennant so beautiful and the life of a shepherd so short?'

However, the view along the ridge over the rocky 655m (2148ft) top of Moel yr Ogof ('the Hill of the Cave') and the looming bulk of Moel Hebog beyond remind you there is still work to be done, although the shallow col and brief climb to **Moel yr Ogof** passes easily enough.

Legend has it that the **cave of Moel yr Ogof's name** is one of many reputedly used as hiding places by the Welsh national hero Owain Glyndwr, the charismatic leader of a 15th-century rebellion against the rule of the English king, Henry IV. Although defeated and hunted no one knows what became of him after the uprising failed. He simply vanishes from the pages of history, never caught and never to be heard of again.

There is nothing for it but to set the brain in neutral while the body gets on with hauling itself up the curving, bald flank of the mountain.

From the summit, a rugged twin of Moel Lefn, the path descends over rock terraces, passing two black pools and then dropping down through a natural chasm to reach the col. From here the onward route up the slopes of **Moel Hebog** is starkly obvious. ◄

The climb is rewarded by yet more excellent views from the somewhat battered trig point before the path heads off southwards to another smaller cairn overlooking **Cwmystradllyn**. From here the ridge is clear enough though largely pathless but with the lake soon in view it is easy to work your way down the slope. The easiest way is slightly to the left, bringing a line of ladder stiles which lead deviously down to a green lane in the valley floor. Follow this rightwards through various gates to eventually reach the house at **Tyddyn Mawr**, where you turn left back to the car park by the dam.

WALK 22

Mynydd Mawr

Start/Finish	Rhyd-Ddu car park SH 571 526
Distance	10km (6 miles)
Total ascent	550m (1800ft)
Grade	Moderate
Time	3–4hr
Terrain	Forest road, clear tracks, steep ridge
Map	OS OL17 Snowdon/Yr Wyddfa
Access	Rhyd-Ddu is on the A4085 Beddgelert to Caernarvon road and is also served by the Welsh Highland Railway
Parking	Pay and display car park by railway station

Any peak that can stand next to Snowdon yet still claim the name 'the Big Hill' – Mynydd Mawr – deserves to be climbed. And it does, providing a varied route of forest tracks and steep ridges to a magnificent viewpoint taking in almost all the major peaks of Snowdonia.

From the car park walk into the village, passing the Cwellyn Arms, to take the left hand turning to Nantlle. Just after leaving the village and passing the speed de-restriction signs take an unmade forest track on the right, signed 'Rhyd-Ddu'. ▶

There is more parking by the junction if needed.

The road traverses the hillside through the trees until it comes to a more open area, where Snowdon comes into view as well as the more rounded top of Moel Eilio across the waters of **Llyn Cwellyn** below.

When the road ends at a turning circle carry on along the now much narrower track across the hillside until it meets a narrow path coming up from the valley, followed by a fork. Here go left and begin climbing. The path emerges from the trees at a ladder stile, where the Nantlle Ridge comes into view. Over the stile the path

Looking down a gully on Craig y Bera to the Nantlle road

turns right to follow the fence making for the ridge ahead with the pinnacles of **Craig y Bera** silhouetted on the skyline.

Once at the ridge the path begins steeply and soon gets steeper, aiming for the left hand side of a wood where it crosses a stile before beginning the even steeper climb to the subsidiary summit of Foel Rudd. The compensation is in the ever-expanding view, especially of the dramatic northern cwms and crags of the Nantlle Ridge across the valley, in comparison with which even Snowdon looks almost tame.

The track crosses the summit of Foel Rudd almost unnoticed as the huge heather and scree-filed bowl of Cwm Planwydd opens up at your feet with Mynydd Mawr itself clearly in view ahead.

With the hard work now behind you the path traverses round the rim of this great void. At one point the ridge becomes very slender with two almost vertical gullies, lined with turrets and pinnacles plunging down towards the buildings of Drws-y-Coed in the valley below. ◀ From here carry on circling the rim of the cwm and on easily up to the summit of **Mynydd Mawr**.

This is a very dramatic moment.

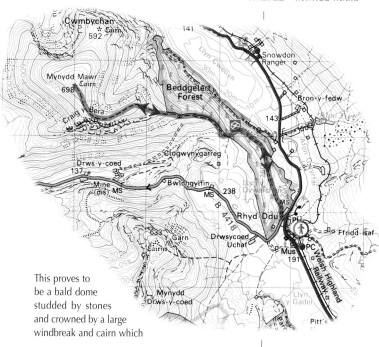

This proves to
be a bald dome
studded by stones
and crowned by a large
windbreak and cairn which

Looking to the Nantlle Ridge

Welsh dragon flies over Mynydd Mawr's summit windbreak

on my last visit sported a Welsh flag. The views are exceptional, from the sea in the west round to take in Moel Eilio and its neighbours with the Glyderau and Carneddau beyond, Tryfan, Snowdon, the Moelwyns, the hills of Cwm Pennant and in the foreground the Nantlle Ridge.

If Mynydd Mawr has a flaw it is that it lends itself neither to a circular walk nor a horseshoe and the most attractive return is to retrace your steps back around the rim and down the ridge – which feels almost steeper in descent than ascent – and back down to the forest road.

WALK 23

Nantlle Ridge

Start	Rhyd-Ddu SH 572 527
Finish	Cors y Llyn SH 488 499
Distance	13km (8 miles)
Total ascent	1025m (3363ft)
Grade	Moderate
Time	5–6hr
Terrain	Steep climb to start then narrow ridges with a little mild scrambling
Map	OS OL17 Snowdon/Yr Wyddfa
Access	Rhyd-Ddu is on the A4085 Beddgelert to Caernarfon road and also served by a station on the Welsh Highland Railway. Cors y Llyn is reached by turning off the A487 Porthmadog to Caernarfon road to Nebo. At the school in the centre of the village turn up Ffordd y Llyn towards the rocky cwm of Dulyn. At a right hand bend after a fifth of a mile a gravel road turns downhill leftwards to a small rough car park below the outfall of the lake.
Parking	Start: national park pay and display car park. Finish: small gravel car park off the road by Llyn Cwm Dulyn
Notes	Although the ridge presents no great technical difficulties in good weather there are exposed sections which are best avoided in high winds; under snow and ice the walk becomes a much more serious proposition

The Nantlle Ridge is without doubt one of the finest day's walking to be had anywhere in Wales and in many people's opinion is second only to the Snowdon Horseshoe as a ridge walking experience. It is best enjoyed as a full traverse, as described here. However, that does require either two vehicles, with one left at the far end, or a willing chauffeur to deliver and collect you. If neither can be arranged the ridge is still worth doing as a two-way trip, turning back wherever time and/or energy levels dictate. It is possible to devise a circular route dropping southwards into Beddgelert Forest but all such deviations are so inferior to the crest of the ridge it seems almost perverse to take them.

Most walkers gearing up in the Rhyd-Ddu car park will have their sights set on either Snowdon or else a gentle circuit of the lake, so set your own course. Cross the road to an elaborately decorated gate and head off on a path of slate chippings crossing the fields. Follow it past a cottage and over a footbridge. At the next junction take the path on the right, which leads up a flight of steps to reach a bend on the Nantlle road, where early risers may find a handful of free parking places.

Y Garn and Mynydd Drws-y-Coed from the valley road

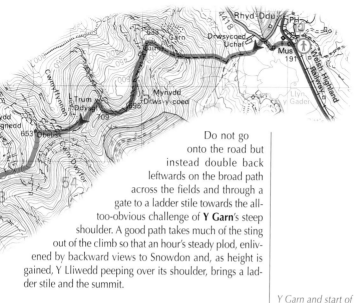

Do not go onto the road but instead double back leftwards on the broad path across the fields and through a gate to a ladder stile towards the all-too-obvious challenge of **Y Garn**'s steep shoulder. A good path takes much of the sting out of the climb so that an hour's steady plod, enlivened by backward views to Snowdon and, as height is gained, Y Lliwedd peeping over its shoulder, brings a ladder stile and the summit.

Y Garn's summit cairn is perched on the very brink of the precipitous north face, with outstanding

Y Garn and start of the Nantlle Ridge from Rhyd-Ddu

The rock turret of Mynydd Drws-y-Coed

views of Mynydd Mawr across the valley. To the south the Pennant hills of Moel Lefn, Moel yr Ogof and Moel Siabod stretch away. But even better than the view is the razor-sharp arête heading over the next peak on the ridge, the soaring rock turret of Mynydd Drws-y-Coed, and then onwards in a line of tops promising unmitigated pleasure to come.

On this next section the path clings in places to the very lip of the slopes, plunging eastwards down over Clogwyn Marchnad, making it a good place to avoid in high winds. The ridge itself demands the use of hands as well as feet though never reaching the technical level of a full-blown scramble and should pose no serious problems for experienced walkers, although a head for heights may well prove useful.

The traverse to **Trum y Ddysgl** begins down grassy slopes but beyond the col the path is soon drawn back towards the crest of the ridge. The summit is broad and grassy, but once the descent to the next peak, **Mynydd Tal-y-Mignedd**, begins the ridge quickly narrows to an exhilaratingly slender neck of grass and rock with the ground falling away steeply on either side.

By contrast the opposite slope is a wide grassy
sweep rising to the unmistakeable summit which is
crowned by a tall stone **obelisk** built to celebrate
the Diamond Jubilee of Queen Victoria in 1897.

With your back against the monument is a good
place to contemplate the final major obstacle, the 230m
(750ft) ascent of the serrated ridge of Craig Cwm Silyn,
the highest point of the ridge, beyond the old drovers'
pass of Bwlch Dros-bern. ▶

This pass was
once used by the
shepherds of Cwm
Pennant to get their
flocks to market
in Caernarfon.

The descent is steep and from the bwlch committed
scramblers may opt to attack the arête head-on, but more
cautious walkers will prefer to take a path which angles
up rightwards to bypass the first band of crags before
climbing back up through the boulders and heather to
the ridge where the routes converge. The path here flirts
with the ridge, occasionally crossing to it for dramatic
glimpses down vertiginous gullies to the huge empty
bowl of Cwm Pennant far below.

From here the cliffs and old mine workings of **Moel
Lefn** stand out clearly, while to the east **Snowdon
and Y Lliwedd** are proudly flanked by the cone of Yr
Aran, which is seen to particularly good effect and
mirrored in the distance to the south by the equally
shapely pyramid of Cnicht.

The path climbs steadily before eventually losing
itself in a confusion of boulders just below the top. **Craig
Cwm Silyn**'s summit is a broad rocky plateau dotted
with incongruous remnants of the days of mining while
unseen below are the climbing grounds of the Cwm Silyn
cliffs. By crossing to a rocky tor on the northern edge it is
possible to peer down to the twin lakes in the bed of the
valley and to look back along the sinuous switchback of
the ridge just travelled and, with the hard work done, to
re-live its pleasures.

Meanwhile to the west are two more tops, Garnedd-
Goch and Mynydd Craig Goch, but by now we have had
the best of what the ridge has to offer. If you are planning

to return via the ridge this is probably the place to do so. The crossing to the summit of **Garnedd-Goch** is straightforward and this marks the easiest descent at this end of the ridge.

Purists may choose to go, literally, the extra mile to Mynydd Craig Goch, but the simplest descent from there would still be to return to Garnedd-Goch.

◄ From Garnedd-Goch's summit cairn a steep path drops down beside a wall, crossing grass and occasional bands of loose boulders. After dropping about 170m (550ft) the path turns sharply right at a pair of cairns and standing stones to begin a long traverse, guided by more upright stones and aiming for the green spur above **Llyn Cwm Dulyn**.

Where it meets a broader path coming in from the right turn left and follow it until it reaches a ladder stile by a gate. Do not cross this but take the fainter path leftwards beside the wall, heading towards the now hidden lake. Where it reaches another ladder stile cross this and go down to a footbridge over the reservoir's outlet to the parking area.

SIABOD AND THE MOELWYNS

Above Rhos Farm on the route above Moel Siabod (Walk 24)

WALK 24
Moel Siabod

Start/Finish	Bryn Glo car park SH 736 570
Distance	11km (7 miles)
Total ascent	730m (2395ft)
Grade	Moderate
Time	4hr
Terrain	Hill paths, a brief avoidable scramble and forest tracks
Maps	OS OL17 Snowdon/Yr Wyddfa and OS OL18 Harlech, Porthmadog and Y Bala
Access	Bryn Glo is on the A5 2km (1 mile) south of Capel Curig
Parking	Car park at Bryn Glo

For those approaching from the east Moel Siabod enjoys a brief spell of fame. As you progress up the A5 from Betws-y-Coed it is the first of the big mountains to come into view, its knobbly ridge drawing the eye and making it centre stage. But it is a brief stardom. Once past the outdoor centre at Plas y Brenin everything changes: the pointed tops of the Snowdon Horseshoe shoulder their way to the front, screaming for attention, and Siabod finds itself slipping into the wings. That's a bit unfair, as Siabod is a fine hill, and also has one of the finest views of Snowdon and its acolytes. A little confusingly, the Ordnance Survey maps give it the name Carnedd Moel Siabod, although it is actually the northern buttress of the group known as the Moelwyns.

As you walk take time to peer over the wall down to the falls and cascades on Afon Llugwy below.

From the car park, where there is a handy café for post-walk refreshments, cross the road and turn right towards Capel Curig. ◄ After a couple of hundred metres turn left over the attractive arch of **Pont Cyfyng**. Walk up the lane. At the houses take the right hand fork up a surfaced lane signed to Moel Siabod. Carry on up the lane until a sharp right hand bend where a broad track goes straight ahead to bypass the buildings of Rhos Farm. After it re-joins the track beyond the farm by a small terrace of holiday cottages the summit of Moel Siabod comes into view across the moor. Climb a stile by a metal gate and carry on up the now rough track, aiming for the peak.

The path continues climbing steadily and unerringly to reach a small but picturesquely set tarn. Pass to the right of this and continue up through quarry spoil heaps, passing to the left of a flooded pit with a couple of attractive waterfalls tumbling into it and press on up the slope.

At the top you are rewarded with the sight of **Llyn y Foel** in the shallow bowl below and the western hills beyond. The path picks its way as best it can through the often boggy ground to the right on the lake and aiming for the rocky ridge of Daear Ddu beyond, seeking what dry ground it can find.

Once the crest is gained there are two distinct options. The pedestrian variation, in every sense of the word, takes a track which rises on the left hand side of the ridge. Those who prefer a more entertaining ascent have the choice of attacking the crest

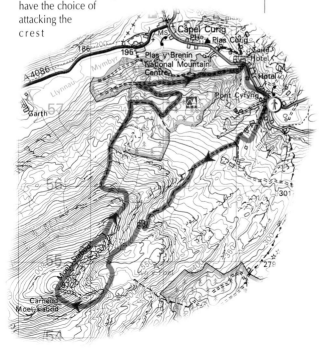

Moel Siabod

directly via a series of enjoyable and fairly easy slabs, grooves, walls and pinnacles closer to the rim of the cwm. The routes meet on the main ridge leading to the top of **Moel Siabod**, where the final slope climbs beside a fence to the summit rocks.

> The views from **Moel Siabod's summit** are second to none, with the sharp tops of the Snowdon Horseshoe, the great humps of the Glyderau, the rocky turrets of Tryfan and the domes of the Carneddau stretched across the horizon.

From the trig point and a large circular windbreak head off north east down the summit ridge to a grassy col where the path heads down leftwards in a more northerly direction over a maze of low rocks. The path is easily lost at this point amid the jumble of boulders but don't worry, it is equally quickly rediscovered once the rocks have been crossed and the turf resumes. It angles down across the hillside, making for the distant buildings of **Capel Curig**: if they cannot be picked out aim for the far (eastern) end of the twin lakes of **Llynnau Mymbyr** below.

Daer Ddu Ridge

Follow the path over double stiles and then across a more boggy section followed by rocks, until a block of forestry appears ahead. Carry on down the path heading for the trees, crossing two stiles to enter the woodland. Where it joins a wider track turn right and shortly after, at a junction on a bend, take the left hand, lower option. The path drops gently until it reaches a barrier. Go past this, ignoring a turning down to the left and a hundred metres or so further on trend rightwards through another barrier. Stay on the path until shortly after a flight of stone steps the path divides. The left hand branch crosses a footbridge to the main road and a pub if you are desperately thirsty, but the right hand branch carries on following the river downstream, traversing more open ground to a footbridge. ▶ Cross the bridge and turn left up onto a vehicle track to arrive back at **Pont Cyfyng**. Turn right down the road to reach the Bryn Glo car park and café.

Having escaped the trees this more open section offers fine views back up to the summit of Moel Siabod.

131

WALK 25
Aberglaslyn Gorge and Llyn Dinas

Start/Finish	Beddgelert SH 591 482
Alternative start	Nantmor SH 597 462
Distance	8km (5 miles)
Total ascent	550m (1800ft)
Grade	Moderate
Time	3–4hr
Terrain	Riverside paths and mountain tracks, one steep descent
Map	OS OL17 Snowdon/Yr Wyddfa
Parking	By the railway station (pay and display) or in a free car park on the Caernarfon road

Beddgelert is a picturesque little village, its business now firmly centred on catering for tourists with its streets lined with pubs, cafés and hotels. This relatively low level walk is sheer pleasure and well worth doing at any time but provides a particularly handy option for a short day or when the higher tops are shrouded in cloud.

Should Beddgelert be bulging at the seams the walk passes a pay and display car park at Nantmor, which makes a handy alternative starting point.

From the Porthmadog side of the bridge in the centre of the village follow a lane signed to Gelert's Grave, heading downstream in front of a row of craft shops and cafés. Ignore the first footbridge and carry on down the side of the river, following a concrete path until it meets the railway line.

It is possible to make a short diversion to visit the **probably mythical grave** that gives the village its name and is its biggest attraction. According to legend, Gelert was a faithful hound belonging to Prince Llewelyn. One day the prince went hunting without the dog and returned to find Gelert covered in

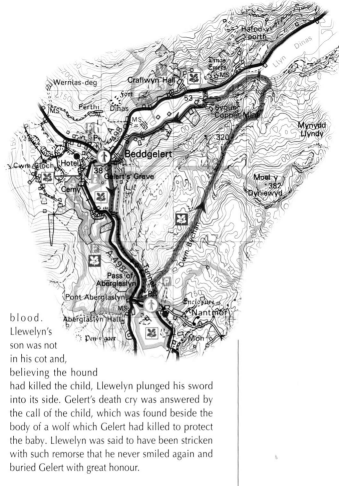

blood. Llewelyn's son was not in his cot and, believing the hound had killed the child, Llewelyn plunged his sword into its side. Gelert's death cry was answered by the call of the child, which was found beside the body of a wolf which Gelert had killed to protect the baby. Llewelyn was said to have been stricken with such remorse that he never smiled again and buried Gelert with great honour.

Cross the footbridge over the river and then immediately go through a kissing gate to cross the line. ▶ Carry on down the path, now following the opposite bank.

Take care to watch out for trains.

The **Welsh Highland Railway** has its roots firmly in the days of the slate quarries that riddled these hills, as it was built to transport valuable stone, but these days the restored line makes its living carrying visitors the picturesque 40km (25 miles) from Caernarfon to Porthmadog.

This is the start of an enchanting section along a narrow path which hugs the waterside. The pitching work attests to its popularity with walkers and picnickers alike, while the song of the river dropping over a series of cascades drowns the sound of any cars using the road on the opposite bank. The whistle of the restored railway in the gorge only adds to the other worldly charm of the route.

All too soon the path reaches a lane close to **Nantmor**. Do not go onto this but instead take a narrow path climbing leftwards up the slope and then meandering through trees to reach a National Trust car park. ◀

This is the walk's alternative start.

From the car park take a track passing through a tunnel under the railway line to a picnic area and follow the signs to **Cwm Bychan**. The route climbs through mixed woodland of oak and silver birch, with the quiet of the trees in marked contrast to the boisterous tumult of the playful river on the earlier section. At the top

Remains of Cwm Bychan's ropeway and spoil heaps

Llyn Dinas

of the first steep slope a handily placed bench invites walkers to linger for a few minutes to recover their breath while enjoying the view back down the valley to the distant sea.

The path continues through a shallow valley flanked by bracken, heather and rocky outcrops before reaching the remnants of the old copper mine cableway which once served these slopes. A line of pylons and a wheel testify to the scale of the operations once carried out here.

At a fork in the path take the right hand branch aiming for a low col ahead. As the path crosses the watershed it climbs a ladder stile and the Snowdon massif appears ahead, with the blue waters of Llyn Dinas visible in the valley below. The path contours leftwards to a three-armed marker post. Resist the invitation to head directly back to Beddgelert and instead turn right steeply downhill to **Llyn Dinas**.

At the lakeside turn left through a kissing gate to follow a narrow path beside the river. When it reaches a road turn left towards the **Sygun Copper Mine**, but at the entrance carry on rightwards along the lane. ▸ As it

Although tarmacked this stretch is a pleasure, passing through woods and between hedgerows.

135

Beddgelert is a picturesque village

nears the main road do not cross the bridge but instead take a kissing gate on the left to follow the well-made path beside the water all the way back to the green and its brightly coloured houses before reaching **Beddgelert** Bridge.

WALK 26
Cnicht and Cwm Croesor

Start/Finish	Croesor SH 632 447
Distance	12km (7 miles)
Total ascent	650m (2132ft)
Grade	Moderate
Time	4–5hr
Terrain	Hill tracks, boggy in places
Maps	OS OL17 Snowdon/Yr Wyddfa and OS OL18 Harlech, Porthmadog and Y Bala
Access	Croesor is reached by a 2 mile single track road from Garreg on the A4085 between Beddgelert and Penrhyndeudraeth (the turning is marked 'Plas Brondan gardens')
Parking	National park car park in the village

The isolated village of Croesor, at the end of a long, blind valley was once home to the men who worked the slate quarries further up the mountain. Between the 1850s and its closure in the 1930s local quarries produced 2000 tons of high quality slate a year for everything from billiard table tops to grave stones and ornamental stonework. The slate was taken down the valley to Penrhyndeudraeth to be loaded on the Ffestiniog railway.

Throughout the approach from the main road the pyramid of Cnicht is almost constantly in view, beckoning you on. Despite its comparatively low height of 689m (2260ft) the mountain, nicknamed 'the Matterhorn of Wales', is one of the national park's most striking peaks and its name is said to be derived from an old word for knight because its pointed summit resembles a warrior's helmet.

From the car park in the village turn right up between the houses and, where the road ends at a cottage and deteriorates into a slate-surfaced track, go straight ahead through the metal gate and carry on uphill. Go through a second gate to the top of the slope, where a signed

Cnicht's surprising summit ridge

footpath to Cnicht bears off to the right to begin the climb across the moor to the ridge.

At a wall corner the path takes a sharp right by another waymarker post.

> The **waymarking** is little short of lavish, although it is a little ironic that the route to one of the most unmistakable summits in the national park should also be one of the best marked.

Climb to a ladder stile and cross this onto the ridge proper, turning left towards the summit. After a last steep pull through a final rock band the path arrives at the very pinnacle of **Cnicht**, which suddenly proves itself to be something of an imposter.

> The **perfect pyramid** that has lured you forwards throughout the approach turns out to be not the expected sharp summit at all but the gable end of a hummocky ridge. Nevertheless it has a real eagle's perch view, especially when looking to the south where the ground drops away sharply

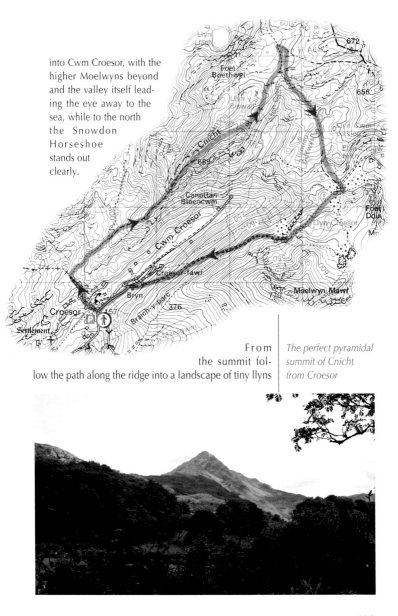

into Cwm Croesor, with the higher Moelwyns beyond and the valley itself leading the eye away to the sea, while to the north the Snowdon Horseshoe stands out clearly.

From the summit follow the path along the ridge into a landscape of tiny llyns

The perfect pyramidal summit of Cnicht from Croesor

Old quarry buildings at Croesor

This next section is unmitigated joy to walk descending a clear path and then deep cushioning turf.

and abandoned quarries. ◄ Carry on down to the col by **Llyn yr Adar**, easily recognised by its tiny central island, and look out for a cairn on the right marking the start of a path leading off around the head of the cwm.

This makes a slowly descending traverse, by turns clear and then indistinct, until it reaches two small lakes where the ground becomes very soggy. Those who wish to emerge dryshod should stay as high as they can rather following the established path through the bog.

Soon a substantial group of abandoned quarry buildings come into view ahead and slightly left, while away to the right on the opposite slope a large flattened area of spoil marks the remains of the old Croesor Quarry, with a green rake dropping away from it. This will be the return route to the village. However first of all make your way towards the first set of quarry buildings.

During the last century this area echoed to the clamour of hardy men wresting slate from the earth. Today all that remains are **roofless ruins** with dangerously leaning walls, inhabited only by ghosts and sheep, the sounds of industry replaced by the cronk of ravens.

The crumbling buildings, which are being slowly reclaimed by the mountain, are to be explored only with the utmost caution.

From this point it would be easy to include the summit of Moelwyn Mawr (see Walk 27) which towers above but, having made the mini masterpiece of Cnicht the focus of this walk, it seems almost inappropriate to let the bullying bigger brother muscle in and spoil the nigh perfect scale of this half day outing. So from behind the extreme right hand end of the buildings take the faintest of tracks which climbs up diagonally rightwards below the spoil heaps. It soon reaches a ladder stile which seems to have been expertly placed in the boggiest position possible.

Climb over then scuttle swiftly rightwards along the fence for a few feet to higher and drier ground, switching after a couple of hundred metres to climb diagonally rightwards, again up a path which becomes steadily clearer as it enters more quarry workings. The path squeezes between two very substantial slate walls to pass the diminutive **Llyn Croesor** before continuing its rising traverse to emerge above the ruins of Croesor Quarry. ▶ Drop down to this and climb another ladder stile at the start of the tramway down the valleyside. The track weaves pleasantly down to join a lane leading back to the car park at the end of near perfect walk to a fine top, wild moorland and a taste of rugged industrial history.

The quarry was seen earlier from the other side of the valley.

WALK 27

The Moelwyns

Start/Finish	Croesor SH 632 447
Distance	10km (6 miles)
Total ascent	780m (2559ft)
Grade	Moderate
Time	4–5hr
Terrain	Mainly grassy paths, wet at the end
Map	OS OL18 Harlech, Porthmadog and Y Bala
Access	Croesor is reached by a 2 mile single track road from Garreg on the A4085 between Beddgelert and Penrhyndeudraeth (the turning is marked 'Plas Brondan gardens')
Parking	National park car park in the village

The Moelwyns will never appeal to those who like their mountains pristine: they have been bashed about far too much for that. Although today the crests and cwms are often deserted they once rang to the clamour of industry, especially quarrying. The village of Croesor is dominated by the two summits of Moelwyn Mawr ('Big White Mountain') at 770m (2526ft) and Cnicht at 698m (2290ft), and for once it is the junior partner that stands more proudly. Cnicht's perfect pyramid is a magnet for the eye throughout the approach to the village and dominates the view from it. Moelwyn Mawr, by contrast, seems like a grassy lump.

But Moelwyn Mawr and its little sister, Moelwyn Bach (just 60m (196ft) lower) are no poor relations to their more glamorous neighbour. They offer beautiful walking on green ridges which are magnificently secluded and sufficiently isolated to offer superb views back into the high mountains and out to the coast. If desired all three could be visited in a single walk by starting up Cnicht (Walk 26) and linking with this walk at Croesor Quarry.

From the car park take a path in the far right hand corner. Go out onto the delightful, tree-lined lane and turn left up the valley. When the tarmac runs out at a fork by a row of

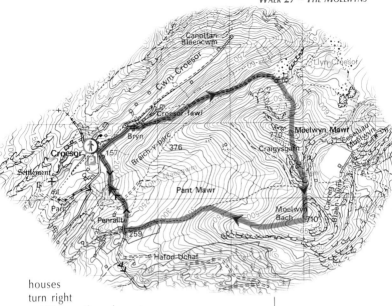

houses
turn right
uphill to go through a gate
to join a broad quarry track which climbs steadily across
the hillside for 2km (1¼ miles). At the top of the rake the
path arrives at the disused Croesor Quarry with its collection of ruins. Behind the buildings a path climbs the
grass slope towards the crags, angling initially rightwards
before cutting back left.

> The men who rived the **slate** from the mountains are
> now long gone but the diggers and delvers have left
> their mark all over these hills in the form of melan-
> choly abandoned buildings, huge collapsing craters
> and vast heaps of spoil scattered across the slopes.
> The buildings, for the most part now roofless, are
> gradually collapsing back into the earth. Many,
> like the quarries and tunnels themselves, are in a
> dangerous condition and best avoided. A patient
> Nature is slowly reclaiming the tips but it will be
> many a long year before the scars are healed.

The intermittent path weaves its way up damply to pass to the right of the largest rocky knoll, where the various strands that have proved so elusive below merge into a clearer track heading towards a ladder stile. Do not cross this but instead turn up the great arc of the ridge to the summit of **Moelwyn Mawr**.

The **views across to Snowdon** are superb, although as you gain height the factories and spoil heaps of Blaenau Ffestiniog, soon joined by the buildings of the former Trawsfynydd nuclear power station on its lake, are a rather less beautiful addition to the panorama. The quickest glance in their direction explains that strange 'hole' in the middle of any map of the national park, where the boundary neatly snips out Blaenau.

Leaning against the square trig point and with your back to the unwelcome intrusion, the vista takes on a more natural look to the Aberglaslyn Estuary and the sands of Tremadog Bay.

Craigysgafn and Moelwyn Bach

To the south is the rocky ridge linking the summit with Moelwyn Bach. To reach it retrace your steps for a hundred metres or so and then take the clear path towards the ridge of **Craigysgafn**.

This intervening **mini-summit**, every bit as rocky as Moelwyn Mawr was grassy, is studded with bands of gleaming white quartz while below the waters of Llyn Stwlan glitter. The level of this lake rises and falls dramatically on a daily basis because it is the upper reservoir for a hydro-electric pump storage power station, a smaller and less modern version of the huge Dinorwig 'Electric Mountain' station buried deep inside Elidir Fawr above Llanberis (Walk 12). Unwanted off-peak electricity is used to pump water from the lower lake to this higher reservoir from which it can be unleashed through the turbines to create instant power at periods of high demand.

The rugged slopes of Rhinog Fawr

At the final col of Bwlch Stwlan do not be tempted by the broad track heading leftwards. Instead take the slender and much fainter grassy track heading up the ridge towards the daunting crags. However, it quickly veers left to climb diagonally up the scree and outflank the rocks, arriving between **Moelwyn Bach**'s two summits. Turn right to the higher, northern, one.

◄ The path sticks to the ridge aiming for the right hand edge of a long finger of conifer plantation in the valley below. The final flat section before the trees is boggy as the path picks its way gingerly through the reeds to enter the plantation via the right hand end, following the edge of the trees to reach a narrow lane. Turn right along this gated road and follow it all the way back to Croesor.

The grassy slopes just below the top make an ideal lunch stop from which to contemplate the long, easy descent of the west ridge from Moelwyn Bach towards the sea.

THE RHINOGS

Climbing the Roman Steps (Walk 28)

WALK 28

Rhinog Fawr by the Roman Steps

Start/Finish	Cwm Bychan SH 645 315
Distance	8km (5 miles)
Total ascent	610m (2000ft)
Grade	Moderate
Time	4–5hr
Terrain	An historic paved route followed by untracked slopes
Map	OS OL18 Harlech, Porth Madog and Bala
Access	Turn off the A496 at Llanbedr between Barmouth and Harlech and follow the signs for Cwm Bychan, the road eventually becoming single track to arrive after 5 miles at Cwm Bychan
Parking	In a field at the farm at Cwm Bychan (fee)

The Rhinogs have a reputation for being among the most rugged mountains in all of Wales – and it is richly deserved. They display impressive amounts of naked rock on almost every side and are clothed in deep, dense heather which is Heaven to behold in bloom but can be Hell to plough through on the broad untracked slopes. Happily, this superb ascent makes use of an historic pathway that smooths the way to the summit of the higher of the two mountains that give the range its name. It should be said that the same route also provides probably the best line of descent but for those who insist on a circular route and are willing to suffer a little for the privilege it includes a descent by the unfrequented Gloyw Lyn.

Go through the gate at the top of the top of the car park and turn right up the broad path through broadleaf woodland of sessile oak trees – a continuation of the delightful landscape you have traversed to reach **Cwm Bychan** – to reach the foot of the **Roman Steps**.

The origin of these **hundreds of gritstone flags** is mysterious but, despite its name, it is generally

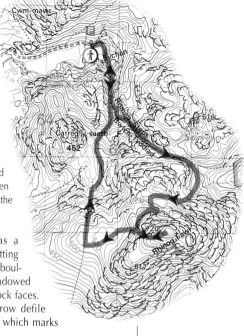

agreed among historians that the Romans had little part to play in the construction of this once-vital track through these inhospitable mountains. More likely that it was a mediaeval trade route used to carry goods between the inland valleys and the coast.

The path climbs as a clear, unmissable line cutting through the wilderness of boulders and heather overshadowed on all sides by tiers of rock faces. Carry on through a narrow defile to reach **Bwlch Tyddiad**, which marks

Passing Llyn Du

the top of the track and opens out views across the vast forests beyond. Begin to drop down the other side, but after about 100m look out for a narrow path heading up through the heather. ◄ Eventually the two join and climb to the dark, sheltered waters **Llyn Du**, a high tarn in a crag-shadowed hollow. Scramble and boulder hop around the right hand side of the lake to reach a drystone wall where the path turns sharply leftwards to clamber uphill following the line of the wall. As it climbs to a shoulder look down to the right for the elongated shape of Gloyw Lyn, whose waters are a key landmark on the circular return. When the path begins to turn downhill a faint but rapidly improving path breaks off uphill to climb **Rhinog Fawr**'s final slopes. Take note of the various junctions as they will be needed on the descent.

It is possible to drop a little lower down the pass to an easier path at the cost of losing a little more height.

Just before the top is reached the rocky duo of **Rhinog Fach and Y Llethr**, separated by the high lake of Llyn Howell, appear to the right. Unusually, the Rhinogs that give their name to the range are not the highest peaks: that honour falls to Y Llethr at 756m (2480ft). The Rhinogs themselves weigh in at only third and fourth places, Rhinog Fawr at

Rhinog Fach and Y Llethr

Rough walking in the Rhinogs

720m (2362ft) and Rhinog Fach 712m (2335ft) after second-placed Diffwys at 750m (2460ft).

The summit presents a tremendous panorama of hills encompassing a sweep of upland all the way from the Lleyn Peninsula, across the great arc of Snowdonia to Cadair Idris in the south.

From the top the easiest descent is to retrace your steps all the way to the car, but a complete circular route is more satisfying: head towards **Gloyw Lyn**, and aim for a gate in the drystone wall. The gate is most easily located by tracing the line of the path coming towards it across the moor from the south west. Once through this the choice of routes – though both are virtually trackless – is either to head downhill, following the bed of an initially shallow valley, or to accompany the wall uphill to reach the spur. Here a vague and intermittent line of gently angled slabs, interspersed with the clinging heather and hidden boulders for which the Rhinogs are justly infamous, winds its way down to the lake. ▶

Go round the right hand side and look out for a faint path heading down into the valley. This becomes more established as it gathers other paths to it, winding between heathery knolls, eventually rejoining the flagged **Roman Steps** path used on the outward leg.

Once you reach the lake the worst of the heather-bashing is over.

WALK 29
Rhinog Fach and Y Llethr

Start/Finish	Nantcol SH 641 269
Distance	13km (8 miles)
Total ascent	740m (2428ft)
Grade	Strenuous
Time	5–6hr
Terrain	Rocky paths and high ridges with two steep climbs
Map	OS OL18 Harlech, Porthmadog and Y Bala
Access	From the A496 Harlech–Barmouth road turn off at Llanbedr and follow signs to Nantcol. Coming from the south you could turn off at Dyffryn Ardudwy, but this entails opening and closing an endless succession of gates.
Parking	Car park a few yards beyond Maes-y-Garnedd farm (small fee). It may be tempting to park near Cil-cychwyn, where the path rejoins the road, but the rash of no parking signs around the buildings is not inviting.

The Rhinogs are renowned for their demanding terrain, often involving trekking through ankle-snagging heather harbouring hidden boulders. This circuit, taking in the lower of the two Rhinogs and visiting the highest point of the range, is something of an exception, with almost every step on clear and well-established paths, while the dramatic ridges and beautifully situated mountain lakes make it not merely a day to be savoured but one to be remembered.

The views open up as you **drive up from the coast road** with the three peaks of Rhinog Fawr, Rhinog Fach and Y Llethr dominating the scene with the notch of Bwlch Drws Ardudwy clearly visible between the two Rhinogs.

Today the farmhouse of Maes-y-Garnedd is peaceful enough but it has a bloody walk-on part

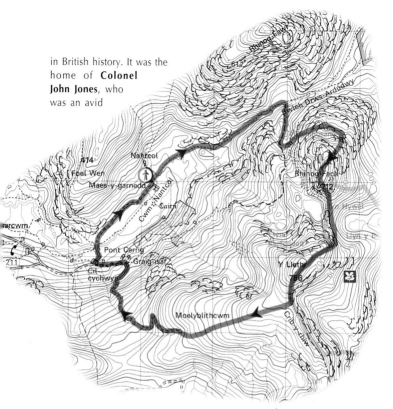

in British history. It was the home of **Colonel John Jones**, who was an avid

Republican during the English Civil War. He was one of the signatories to the death warrant of King Charles I and served Cromwell in Ireland during the ruthless suppression of the population there. However, with the Restoration of Charles II his actions caught up with him and he suffered the agonising traitor's death of being hanged, drawn and quartered.

Behind **Maes y Garnedd** car park is a small pool. Cross the stream below it on stepping stones and begin a long, gently rising ascent of the cwm on an ancient trackway which, like the more famous Roman Steps (Walk 28) in neighbouring Cwm Bychan, is partially paved. It also

Climbing the heather gully to the north top

makes use of the natural stone bedding planes but still has the occasional wet section.

After about an hour the track reaches a prominent finger of rock, streaked with quartz, just before a narrow defile. Below and to the right a ladder stile crosses the wall. This is the start of a path heading eventually to Llyn Hywel and gives a more direct ascent of Rhinog Fach. However, if you want to visit the isolated tarn of **Llyn Cwmhosan** carry on a short way to a flat, marshy area with a second ladder stile on the far side. ◀ From the stile a steep, narrow path climbs abruptly up through the bracken, heather and boulders to the lake.

It can be crossed directly, or a drier alternative circles round the far end of the marsh and cuts back to the stile that way.

At Llyn Cwmhosan go down the right hand side of the lake and climb a heathery knoll, with fine views back across the water to Rhinog Fawr, to join the path coming up from the first ladder stile. Continue on to where another path comes in from the right and 150 metres further on a faint track forks away left towards the western slopes of Rhinog Fach and a large grassy slab which divides two broad fans of scree. Before reaching the slab a narrow path breaks off uphill aiming to the left of the left hand fan of scree and onwards to the ridge.

The climb is every bit as steep as it looks but, though thigh-burningly sharp, it is also mercifully fairly short and emerges on the ridge by the north top, with views out ahead over the smothering green carpet of conifers of the Coed-y-Brenin Forest below. From here the walk to the 712m (2335ft) summit of **Rhinog Fach** is a delightful stroll along the undulating ridge to the cairn.

This is a **superb vantage point** from which to admire the crumpled rock formations of Rhinog Fawr and to appreciate just how much naked rock is on show and why these comparatively lowly hills offer such rough walking. To the south is the great bulk of Y Llethr, at 756m (2480ft) the highest of the Rhinogs, across the deep cleft which hides Llyn Hywel.

Drop back down to the path which traverses just below the eastern side of the ridge and comes to a ladder stile over a wall. Almost immediately it crosses a second stile going briefly forwards before curling leftwards over rock and scree, with the idyllically situated **Llyn Hywel** now visible below.

Rhinog Fach and Llyn Hywel

Stunning views back to Rhinog Fach and Rhinog Fawr compensate for the route's steepness.

From the col the path climbs steeply to the right of the wall following a clear but unforgivingly steep path. ◀ It finally emerges on **Y Llethr**'s summit ridge, which comes as a surprise after so many hours among such dramatically rocky terrain.

The **highest point in the rugged Rhinogs** is actually a broad green field bisected by an immaculate drystone wall running along the crest. The wall has obviously absorbed all the available stone and the summit is marked by an almost embarrassingly modest cairn but the views are superb. Cadair Idris appears to the south, the Mawddach Estuary stretches away to Cardigan Bay while the next peak of Diffwys promises adventures for another day. The upturned pudding basin dome of Moelfre dominates to the west.

From the summit follow the wall down the ridge to a wall corner with two ladder stiles. Cross the stile going straight ahead but turn immediately right beside the wall, following the faint path for about a mile. Where the wall turns right follow it downhill, ignoring the first gap to reach a gate about 400 metres from the corner. Go through this and look down and left to a rough vehicle track which curls down beside the wall. Follow it as it meanders lazily down to a farmhouse and turn down the concrete access track to the valley road at **Cil-cychwyn** and return right along the road. This is where it might have been welcome to park your vehicle but the farm buildings are liberally plastered with No Parking signs and roadside spots are conspicuous by their absence so there is little for it but to hike the last mile along the tarmac to the road head at **Maes-y-Garnedd** and enjoy the dramatic view of the Rhinogs ahead.

DOLGELLAU, CADAIR IDRIS AND THE SOUTH

Lunch on Penygadair, with Cwm Cau below and Mynydd Pencoed beyond (Walk 31)

WALK 30

Precipice Walk, Dolgellau

Start/Finish	Coed y Groes car park SH 746 212
Distance	5km (3 miles)
Total ascent	70m (230ft)
Grade	Easy
Time	2hr
Terrain	Well-marked, mostly level paths
Map	OS OL18 Harlech, Porthmadog and Y Bala (not that you'll really need it)
Access	From Dolgellau take the A494 towards Bala and turn off left to Llanfachreth: Coed y Groes car park is on the left just after the brow of the hill
Note	This path has been in use since 1890 by permission of the landowners but in order to prevent it becoming a public right of way it is closed on 1 February each year

This walk has been popular with visitors to the Welsh coast since Victorian times and has lost none of its charm in the intervening century and a quarter. Although it has no pretensions to the summit of its parent hill, Foel Cynwch, this delightful circuit is nevertheless, thanks to its high starting point, a wonderful hill walk. It traces a contour around the mountain and offers ever-changing vistas of Snowdonia, the beautiful Mawddach Estuary and the alluring massif of Cadair Idris to the south. It also represents an enticingly simple stroll, with rewards far exceeding the minimal effort it demands.

All in all it is the perfect antidote to the rigours of Cadair Idris or a rugged day on the neighbouring Rhinogs. It is ideal for a rest day, a family day or merely to rescue a rainy one. It would be easy to gallop around the circuit but to do so would be sacrilege. Take your time and savour it all.

From the top of the car park take the broad path which curls to the right and goes on to join a wider track through mature deciduous woodland and passing along the edge of fields to reach a cottage. Here turn left up

through more woodland
and carry on to where
the delectable sheet
of Llyn Cynwch
comes into
view.

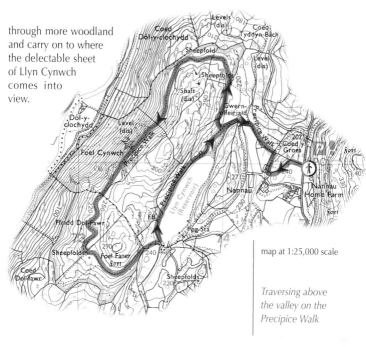

map at 1:25,000 scale

*Traversing above
the valley on the
Precipice Walk*

Llyn Cynwch

Do not progress as far as the lake but instead right turn uphill on a signposted path by the side of a drystone wall. The path quickly levels out, giving beautiful pastoral views of the fields and woods surrounding the village of Llanfachreth to the north east. From here it leads on, maintaining a fairly level course around the mountain offering constantly changing views in return for precious little effort.

At the next bend the ground suddenly drops away, plunging down to the A470 Dolgellau–Trawsfynydd road while ahead the views open out towards the sea. At the end of this '**Precipice Walk**' section the views encompass the Mawddach Estuary. ◄ The path curves round all too soon to reach **Llyn Cynwch**. The path follows the pleasantly wooded left hand bank before rejoining the outward leg back to car park.

A bench has been thoughtfully supplied, so pause and admire the magnificent vista down the river and across to Cadair Idris.

Start/Finish	Ty Nant SH 697 153
Distance	10km (6 miles)
Total ascent	734m (2420ft)
Grade	Moderate
Time	4hr
Terrain	Good paths on the Pony Path, eroded scree if the Foxes Path is used in descent
Map	OS OL23 Cadair Idris and Llyn Tegid
Access	Leave Dolgellau on the road signed to Cadair Idris and follow the narrow road to the national park car park at Ty Nant
Parking	National park pay and display car park

The Pony Path is the longest-established path up Cadair Idris. As its name suggests it was an early packhorse track over the mountain from the south to the market at Dolgellau, and as long ago as Georgian times well-heeled visitors were being led on horseback to the summit where they were plied with refreshments. Today it remains a contender for the most popular route up the mountain, so do not expect to have it to yourself.

From the car park turn right up the road, crossing an attractive little bridge, for about 50 metres and then take the signed Pony Path on your left. The track climbs through mixed deciduous woodland to go through a kissing gate with a poignant memorial to Will Ramsbotham, a Yorkshire runner who in 1993 won the Cadair Idris fell race in record time of 1hr 25min only to die in a climbing accident on the mountain the following day.

For the most part the path needs little description as it makes a rising traverse below the tall crags of Cyfrwy aiming for a steep grassy spur. ▶

As befits a path which has existed for centuries, the way is always clear, either trodden deep into the earth or pitched with stone slabs.

*Penygadair from
Cyfwry col*

The way steepens and
the path climbs in a series of zigzags, at the top of which
it comes to a cluster of gates and stiles marked 'Grid Ref
SH691135'. Take note of this important junction if you
are planning to descend by the same route.

From here carry on leftwards, now at a much more amenable angle and the path climbs on a broad, stony way to where it arrives at a col between Cyfrwy and the rocky summit of **Penygadair**, the highest point of **Cadair Idris**, which is the name given to the entire sprawling massif rather than any individual top.

Climbing the Pony Path up Cadair Idris

> As the path reaches the col it reveals the vast cwm below Penygadair's summit, with the tiny lake of **Llyn y Gadair** in its hollow far below and a magnificent view of the northern cliffs. It also gives a view across to the worn scree slope of the Foxes Path (see below).

Carry on around the rim of the cwm to the top of Penygadair, with spectacular views not only to the surrounding hills but also down to the cliffs of Cwm Cau to the south and the adjacent top of Mynydd Pencoed.

> Just below the summit is a **walkers' refuge**, but be careful about sleeping there. According to legend this summit was the chair of Idris, a giant,

philosopher and poet. Anyone who dares to usurp his position by spending the night here, so it is said, will wake up either a poet or a madman. You have been warned!

A glance at the map will reveal what looks like a perfect circular walk descending the Foxes Path setting off by a pair of cairns a little to the east of the summit and dropping to Llyn y Gadair. Unfortunately the mountain these days has other ideas. In the past this was indeed a good proposition but over the years the path has become treacherously eroded and worn and is now not recommended as a way down. Although it is still used by some there is little pleasure in the section down to the llyn. It is a mixture of bare earth, large boulders and little more than an invitation to a broken leg.

Return to the valley by the **Pony Path**, taking care not to miss the junction by the gates and stiles.

WALK 32

Cadair Idris from Minffordd

Start/Finish	Minffordd national park car park SH 732 116
Distance	10km (6 miles)
Total ascent	975m (3200ft)
Grade	Strenuous
Time	5–6hr
Terrain	Clear path but with a sharp introduction, steep climbs and a sharp eroded descent from Mynydd Moel to finish
Map	OS OL23 Cadair Idris and Llyn Tegid
Access	On B4405, just off junction with A487 Dolgellau–Machynlleth road
Parking	National park pay and display car park

This is a classic and popular way to climb Cadair Idris – and thoroughly deserves to be so. It rises through attractive ancient woodland to a majestic mountain cwm that can hold its own against any in Britain, and then enjoys a high level traverse over three fine peaks before revealing a final surprise. A walk to match any in this book, but one which exacts a high price in effort.

From the car park take the broad level path signed to the tea room and visitor centre down a fine avenue of horse chestnuts. Pass the buildings and then turn right through the gate at the foot of a flight of steps. These climb through delightful woodlands of ancient oaks and beech with a lively beck and waterfalls down to your right.

You will be glad of these distractions and the temptations they offer to stop and admire your surroundings because the steps are a brutally steep beginning to the day. There are allegedly more than 700 of them but you will probably be too busy fighting

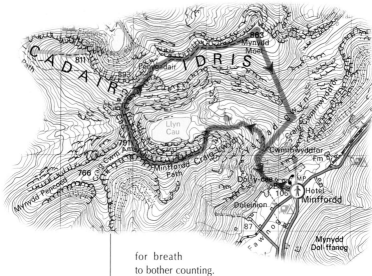

Cadair Idris across Tal-y-Llyn

for breath
to bother counting.
There are certainly plenty, but
console yourself with the thought that at least you
are gaining height quickly.

The start of Cader's 700 (or more!) steps

Finally the path reaches a gate and begins to level off. At a fork take the left hand option, signed to Cwm Cau. ▶ Happily the worst is now behind you and the angle has relented markedly as it climbs gently to arrive at a grassy shelf dotted with boulders.

The other path to Mynydd Moel will be our descent route.

Ahead the triangular peak of **Mynydd Pencoed** dominates the view with the huge cliff of **Craig Cau** tumbling down below it. Already the rocky arms of the cwm begin to enfold you, but for the moment the lake remains hidden as the path makes a rising traverse into the very heart of Cadair.

From the cwm the path begins to climb steeply towards the rim of the corrie and the lake is revealed in the hollow below, almost completely enveloped by steep high walls. This is a truly magnificent place and one to match anything Snowdon or the Glyderau have to offer.

Once the path reaches the shoulder it is worth taking a few paces to the southern edge for views down to Llyn Mwyngil (Tal-y-Llyn) and across the gentler tops of the Tarrens to the mountains of mid-Wales.

Walkers begin the final ridge to Penygadair

Two paths now follow the rim of the cwm, a wider one a few metres below the edge and a narrower one closer to the rim giving dizzying glimpses down to **Llyn Cau** far below and across to the chaos of vegetated rock cascading down from Penygadair, at 893m (2929ft) the highest point of the massif. The path arrives at a ladder stile which delivers you onto the summit of Mynydd Pencoed. From here a clear path drops into a shallow col followed by a stiff and stony pull to the trig point on the summit of **Penygadair**.

There is actually no single summit that carries the title of **Cadair Idris**. The name refers to the huge area of high ground that provides a southern rampart to the Mawddach valley above Dolgellau. The name means Idris' Chair though no one is quite certain who Idris actually was. Some assert he was a national hero, a mighty warrior from the Dark Ages who fought the invading Saxons, while others claim he was a giant, poet and philosopher.

This perhaps is what has given rise to the legend that anyone who sleeps on the summit will awake either a poet or a madman. It is unclear whether passing a nocturnal vigil in the crude refuge a few metres below the highest rocks qualifies for the challenge. From here the views open up northwards across the precipitous face of Cyfrwy and Llyn y Gadair and the northern peaks of Snowdonia down the Mawddach Estuary and out to the railway viaduct at Barmouth.

The next leg of the route stretches away in an easy amble across a broad green saddle to a small rise up to the summit boulders of **Mynydd Moel**. Just before the summit a ladder stile leads over a fence to a large wind shelter and cairn and the final surprise. What has been a gentle grassy dome on the approach now plunges away abruptly at your feet into a deep rocky cwm with **Llyn Arran** like a tiny puddle far below. It makes a suitable finale to the traverse of the highest ridges.

For the descent return to the fence and cross the ladder stile and turn left beside it. The path is faint at first but the fence is an infallible guide. ▶ Where it comes to a ladder stile just as the ground steepens cross this and

The views down into majestic Cwm Cau are especially fine if by now evening light is glinting on the lake.

The summit shelter. Will you emerge as a bard or a madman?

carry on down the other side of the fence to where a path comes in from the right at another ladder stile. Stay on the left hand side of the fence and follow the path down aiming towards a wall.

The path drops steeply, still following the line of the fence, pitched and stepped in places but loose and eroded in others. After a particularly elaborately pitched section it reaches another stile crossing the fence again. Go over this to traverse away rightwards across the slope towards the trees. Cross a stream on a slate bridge and reach the junction of paths passed on the outward leg. All that remains is to follow the path back down the hard-won steps to the car park.

WALK 33
The Dolgoch Falls and Tarrenhendre

Start/Finish	Dolgoch SH 651 047
Distance	10km (6 miles)
Total ascent	600m (1968ft)
Grade	Moderate
Time	4hr
Terrain	Good tracks with a steep start and a very steep descent from the summit
Map	OS OL23 Cadair Idris and Llyn Tegid
Access	From the A487 Dolgellau–Machynlleth road turn onto the B4403 at Minffordd and follow it past Tal-y-Llyn to Dolgoch. The start is also served by the Talyllyn Railway.
Parking	Pay and display car park at the Dolgoch Falls Café

The gentle Tarrens are virtually the last, slightly muted, hurrah of the national park before Snowdonia slips seamlessly into the mountains and valleys of mid-Wales. They will forever lie in the considerable shadow cast by their much higher and dramatic northern neighbour, Cadair Idris, and wisely they make no attempt to compete with that rugged massif. They enjoy no great height nor boast huge crags and cwms, but what they do have is peace and tranquillity in spades. You will be unlucky to find yourself sharing them with more than a handful of others and very probably will have them entirely to yourself – or at least you will once you leave the popular falls behind.

Leave the car park by the tarmac path by the side of the tea rooms and follow it beneath a viaduct that carries the bustling little trains of the Talyllyn narrow gauge railway. The path, maintained as a visitor attraction by the local council, climbs beside the stream and within a few minutes reaches the first of **Dolgoch Falls**, where the stream slides in a double drop through a narrow cleft.

No doubt some will find this opening section a little too touristy but the **falls** are well worth a visit,

Dolgoch's double falls

especially after rain, and any crowds are quickly left behind.

Next comes a climb on a charming path through deciduous woodland of oak, beech and birch mixed with holly and enriched by a series of cataracts and shaded pools as well as the three major falls.

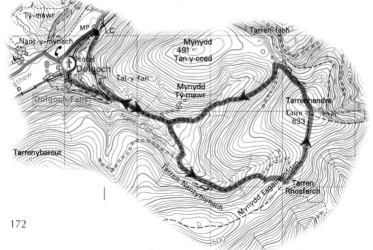

Paths criss-cross the stream but the uphill route remains on the eastern (left) bank, ignoring all diversions and bridges. It climbs past the final fall – another impressive double drop – to reach a footbridge at the summit of the surfaced track. Do not cross this but instead take a rough earthen path still following the stream to escape from the woods by crossing a rudimentary stile onto the open hillside. Here the path climbs up through the rocks and bracken before cutting back leftwards uphill to join a firm vehicle track heading into the valley. Turn right along this.

At a ford cross **Nant Dol-gôch** by a small clapper bridge just below the road or by stepping stones above it where the waterway narrows. Stay on the track as it curls round behind the great green whaleback of Tarrenhendre which is now in front of you.

▶ When the track comes to some sheepfolds with a rusting tin shack briefly turn your back on Tarrenhendre and ford the stream on stepping stones to continue on the vehicle track as it climbs the other side of the valley across the slopes of Tarren Nantymynach.

This is fine country for striding out among these rolling hills that eat up the miles easily.

The open rolling tops of Tarrenhendre

After passing through the last gate the track curls round towards more sheep pens made of corrugated iron. About 200 metres before reaching them a broad track branches off to the right uphill. Follow this as it climbs towards the ridge. It stops a few metres short of the top of the slope but continue up through the heather to the watershed when the views open out over the sinuous curves of the Afon Dyfi/River Dovey below and the low wooded hills beyond. From here a fence is an unerring guide leftwards up the final slopes for the short stroll to **Tarrenhendre**'s summit with a tiny cairn at a fence corner. ◄

From here there are fine views in all directions but especially towards Cadair Idris.

From the summit head off roughly north west on a narrow trod aiming for a nearby junction of fences, which is crossed by a step stile, still following a faint path heading down the left hand side of the fence towards the Tal-y-Llyn valley.

The ground swiftly begins to drop away and the path, still clinging to the fence, plunges downhill, making for some sheep pens on the col below. Here ignore a stile which leads rightwards to drop into the forestry plantations below. From here the map promises a circular outing but it involves descending a precipitously steep gully and complicated navigation through the conifer plantations.

So instead take the track heading away leftwards from the sheep pens. This curves back down the valley of Nant Sychnant to the ford crossed during the ascent. From here turn right back down the valley to either retrace your outward route or, as a variation, ignore the path dropping back down to Dolgoch Falls and instead stay on the vehicle track to follow it all the way back to the main valley road and when you reach the tarmac turn left back to the car park.

BALA

Pistyll Rhaeadr (Walk 38)

WALK 34

Rhobell Fawr

Start/Finish	Llanfachreth SH 756 225
Distance	13km (8 miles)
Total ascent	575m (1900ft)
Grade	Moderate
Time	5hr
Terrain	Woodland paths, some untracked hillside
Map	OS OL23 Cadair Idris and Llyn Tegid and OS OL18 Harlech, Porthmadog and Y Bala
Access	Llanfachreth sits in the fork of the A470 Blaenau–Dolgellau road and the A494 from Bala–Dolgellau and is signposted from both
Parking	Village car park by the school

If anyone ever decided to build the ideal grandstand from which to view most of Snowdonia's mountains the summit of Rhobell Fawr would not be a bad choice. Although only 743m (2408ft) tall, it stands in splendid isolation between Blaenau Ffestiniog, Bala and Dolgellau with no surrounding peaks to overshadow it and so provides one of the most complete panoramas in the national park. Its setting is also charming, its lower slopes cloaked in mixed deciduous woodland that make the approach to the more rugged summit a delight.

From the car park turn right in front of the school and then immediately right again up an enclosed bridleway which leads gently uphill through woodland and pastures. When it reaches the access track to a house on the left jink rightwards through a gate and then immediately left to follow the stony track uphill. When after 100 metres or so the track curls back left towards the house, carry straight on a now much fainter path up to a gate which leads into a felled area. Carry on along the now clearer forestry track for a couple of hundred metres

before going through a gate on the right into an area of enclosed woodland. ▸

The path contours the hillside, passing through a series of gates before joining a stony track coming up the valley. Turn left up this old drove road, aiming for the col in the ridge ahead.

The path leads through a mixture of oak, beech, holly, hazel and the occasional sycamore, with the more rugged upper slopes of Rhobell Fawr ahead.

Summit of Rhobell Fawr

At the top of the pass, **Bwlch Goriwared**, take a ramshackle ladder stile on the right and a faint grassy track which climbs the slope, weaving between knolls and outcrops, guided by the wall to the right.

As you climb the **views open up**. The great northern wall of Cadair Idris dominates the view to the south while to the west the sea appears at the end of the unseen Mawddach Estuary with the chain of the Rhinogs to its north. Further north are the giants of Snowdonia.

The valley to the south contains large blocks of conifers, although in recent years there has been a considerable amount of clear felling.

Eventually the angle relents and the trig point on the summit of **Rhobell Fawr** comes into view, with ever more expansive panoramas, and it is possible to try pick out and name almost every major top as you go round the compass. ◄

From the summit drop down the southern flank to the wall which has been the guide throughout the ascent and work rightwards along it to a ladder stile. From here the faintest of grassy trods weaves its way down through the boulders, generally working its way rightwards, until after crossing a couple of small streams it reaches the boundary wall and follows it steeply downhill to join the forestry road. Turn right along this, passing through a gate and onwards through the former plantation, which is slowly being colonised by nature.

The unmade road leaves the former plantation by a gate next to a group of residual sentinel conifers and after about 300 metres, by some fenced off quarry workings, a signed footpath breaks away rightwards and climbs through a soggy area to meet a wall. Turn left along this and cross a ladder stile in the corner before continuing ahead parallel to the wall on the right but not following it too closely. Within 150 metres a yellow-tipped marker post on the edge of the escarpment signals the descent of a shallow gully. Go down this and, encouraged by the occasional marker post, press on through an area of gorse, bilberry and heather with occasional damp sections until the path re-joins the wall. Here turn left and

follow it to a ladder stile. Go over this and head across another boggy section to climb the short opposite slope before turning left to reach a gate in a wall. Go through this and carry on straight ahead to pass behind a house and then turn left along its access track.

The descent from Rhobell Fawr

This eventually becomes surfaced before reaching a road on the angle of a bend. Turn left along this quiet lane for about 300 metres and then turn right on a signed footpath following the access track of Cae Glas. Just before reaching the house take a stile on the left and continue up the field. Go through an unmarked pedestrian gate in the left hand wall and across a small field to pass below a second farm on a signed diversion to enter woodland, following first of all a small stream and then a wire fence. It leaves the wood at a gate to emerge on the bridleway used on the outward leg. Turn left along this and follow it back to **Llanfachreth**, which is visible in the valley below.

WALK 35

*Cwm Cywarch Horseshoe and
Aran Fawddwy*

Start/Finish	Cwm Cywarch SH 853 187
Distance	12.5km (8 miles)
Total ascent	900m (2950ft)
Grade	Moderate
Time	4–5hr
Terrain	Mountain tracks, wet in places and a steep, rough descent
Map	OS OL23 Cadair Idris and Llyn Tegid
Access	From the A470 Dolgellau to Mallwyd road turn off at Dinas Mawddwy and follow the minor road towards Bala. At Aber-Cywarch turn left to Cwm Cywarch on a single track road to reach Cwm Cywarch in about 4km (2½ miles).
Parking	National park car park (optional donation)

This classic horseshoe to the highest of the Arans can be done in either direction, with each having its adherents. Some prefer the clockwise version to get the steep climb out of the way in ascent but, done this way, the climb towards Aran Fawddwy can be very wet so I prefer to go anti-clockwise to remain dryshod for as long as possible.

Nowadays **Cwm Cywarch** is a peaceful pastoral valley filled with birdsong. However, like many others in the area its past was much more industrial with active lead mines in the hills and mills on the valley floor supporting a much bigger population than it does today.

It was also renowned for its music and was the home of Robert Evans, who in the mid-19th century boasted the name Eos Mawddwy – 'Mawddwy's Nightingale' – for his singing talents.

The magnificent Cwm Cywarch. The route descends the valley

From the car park right turn back down the road for 100 metres to cross a foot-bridge on the left signed 'Aran Ridge Path' and make your way up

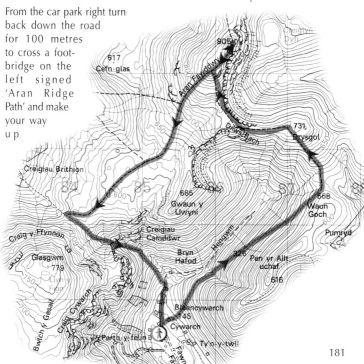

Creglynn Dyfi and the Arans

Admire the dramatic views of the cliffs looming over the farm at Cwm Cywarch. ◄

the initially enclosed track onto the slopes of **Pen yr Allt uchaf**. ◄

It is a long steady flog of more than an hour to a boggy col, where the path meets another coming down from the right. Turn left up this broad track up the grassy slopes of **Drysgol**. The path joins a fence and at a corner it crosses by a ladder stile. Drysgol's nondescript top passes virtually unnoticed before the path curls round the head of Hengwm, with views down rightwards to the small lake of **Creglyn Dyfi** with the craggy east faces of the Arans towering above it.

The path soon joins another fence which follows the ridge round to a small cairn overlooking Hengwm.

The cairn was built as a memorial by the members of an **RAF mountain rescue team** in memory of one of their members, SAC Michael Aspain, who was killed by lightning near this spot while on duty in 1960.

From here continue following the fence line climbing up towards the obvious 905m (2969ft) summit of

Aran Fawddwy. The path crosses the fence by another ladder stile beyond which a faint green trod weaves its way up through boulders to a subsidiary summit and then onwards on a clearer path along the ridge to the unmistakeable main top of Aran Fawddwy, which is marked by a trig point.

From here it is possible to continue the ridge walk by pressing on to the obvious summit of Aran Benllyn, 885m (2901ft) and 2km (1¼ miles) away. The trip there and back will add about 90min and 215m (705ft) of ascent and descent. The traverse of the entire ridge in the opposite direction is described in Walk 36.

From the summit of Aran Fawddwy return to the subsidiary summit passed earlier but pass to the right of it following the fence line. Ignore all the stiles crossing it until you reach a junction of fences with two stiles. Climb the stile on the left, still following the fence downhill. ▶ Carry on across a shallow col and continue to a much more pronounced col, with the steep slopes of Glasgwm ahead and dark shattered cliffs directly below you on the left. Follow the path down into a steep gully below them, following yet another fence and stream past the crag.

When the path reaches the valley floor follow a signed diversion round the farm to join the lane which quickly leads back to the car park.

This is where things start to get rather wet in places though some improvised duckboards in the worst sections make things a little easier.

WALK 36

Traverse of the Aran Ridge

Start	Pont y Pandy, Llanuwchllyn SH 879 298
Finish	Cwm Cywarch GR 853 187
Distance	Full ridge: 15km (9½ miles); to Aran Benllyn and back 12km (8 miles); to Aran Fawddwy and back 16km (10 miles)
Total ascent	1000m (3281ft)
Grade	Moderate
Time	Whole traverse of the ridge (two cars needed) 5hr; to Aran Benllyn and back 4hr; to Aran Fawddwy and back 5–6hr
Terrain	A high mountain ridge, mainly on good paths with an easy scramble
Map	OS OL23 Cadair Idris and Llyn Tegid
Access	From Bala take the A494 to the south western end of Lake Tegid (Bala Lake) and turn left into Llanuwchllyn. Go through the village to the car park just before the bridge.
Parking	Small car park at Pont y Pandy (honesty box); national park car park at Cwm Cywarch (optional donation)

Although not as high as its more famous neighbours to the north, the Aran Ridge is a fine walk, marred only by the difficulty of getting to and from it unless two cars or a willing chauffeur are available for the full traverse. If so you will be in for a magnificent day out, with the bonus of being unlikely to have to share your good fortune with more than a handful of others, if indeed you meet anyone at all. If transport is not available it is possible to still enjoy the edited highlights by following the ridge as far as either Aran Benllyn or, better still, Aran Fawddwy, and then retracing your steps. It is also possible to work out a round trip via Cwm Croes but, in truth, the diversion is so long and the route finding so awkward in places that the circular route does not match the ridge for quality. Better to enjoy this high level outing in both directions.

The ridge path leaves the farm track

From the car park turn left towards the bridge but do not go over it. Instead, cross the road and go through the gate signed Aran Ridge Path. Take the farm track that leads up the valley and at the top of the first rise look out for a stile, again signed Aran Ridge Path, on the right. Cross this and take the bridleway as it climbs initially

map continues on page 187

185

Looking back from Aran Benllyn to Llyn Tegid/Bala Lake

Ahead there are views of the craggy top of Aran Benllyn, the first major summit.

diagonally up the fields to reach the ridge and a stile at the start of open country. In the early stages there are fine views northwards to the Arenigs and backwards along the length of Llyn Tegid. As the bridleway climbs the views keep improving as Snowdon and the Glyderau peep over the intervening ridges. The path continues through a roller-coaster of heather-clad false summits, stiles and soggy cols, the worst of which is crossed on makeshift duckboards.

◄ As the path nears the top it climbs a steep shoulder. At the top of this it is worth diverting to a cairn on the left which marks a view down the west face of the mountain to the dark waters of **Llyn Lliwbran**, cradled in its cwm. Press on past a black pool on the right for the final pull to the quartz-striped rocks of the 885m (2903ft) summit of **Aran Benllyn**, which is crowned by a large cairn.

Here the **views open up towards the sea**, with the massif of Cadair Idris above the Mawddach Estuary. If the full traverse of the ridge is not your goal for the day it would be reasonable to turn back from here but ahead the ridge stretches on towards Aran

Fawddwy, the highest point of the ridge at 905m (2969ft). Including it will add another 4km (2½ miles) and about 90min to the walk.

The walk to **Aran Fawddwy** is a delightful stroll as the path weaves its way in and out of rocky outcrops, for the most part following a fence with the rocky summit, marked by a trig point, clear ahead.

map continues on page 188

Even though it will take less than an hour to make the traverse it is worth another stop here to enjoy the **exceptional views**, with all the major mountain groups in sight and the hills of mid-Wales stretching away in a seemingly endless procession of ridges.

From the summit carry on along the ridge to a subsidiary summit and pass just to its left (east) to pick up a faint grass trod that works its way down through the boulders making for the huge valley of Hengwm.

The path comes to a fence and crosses it via a ladder stile before turning left downhill to the ridge which curls around the rim of **Hengwm**. The onwards descent path descending diagonally the

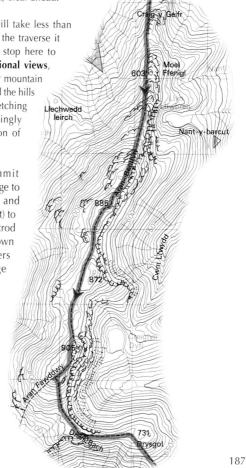

187

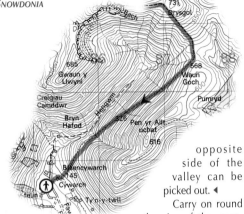

The path passes a poignant memorial cairn to a member of an RAF mountain rescue team who was killed nearby when he was struck by lightning.

opposite side of the valley can be picked out. ◄

Carry on round the rim of the cwm, passing the unremarkable grassy summit of **Drysgol** and cross a fence by a ladder stile. The track runs parallel to the fence down to reach a boggy col where the fence turns off leftwards. Here turn right down into the valley. The path makes a long traversing descent for almost the full length of the valley, the path eventually becoming wider. As it nears the valley floor the track appears to veer leftwards through a gate into a pasture. Look out for a waymarked path breaking off to the right. This continues downhill, becoming enclosed before it crosses a footbridge by a ford to reach the road.

Turn right up the road for about 100 metres to reach the national park car park.

WALK 37

Arenig Fawr and Moel Llyfnant

Start/Finish	Near Llyn Celyn SH 831 392
Distance	16km (10 miles)
Total ascent	850m (2780ft)
Grade	Moderate
Time	5–6hr
Terrain	Mountain tracks, some steep descents and a couple of trackless sections
Map	OS OL18 Harlech, Porthmadog and Bala
Access	From the A4212 Bala to Trawsfynydd road turn off at Pont Rhyd y Fen 1 mile beyond the eastern end of Llyn Celyn: after a mile park on waste ground by a large disused quarry
Parking	On waste ground at roadside

Arenig Fawr is a mountain that deserves to be better known and more travelled. As well as laying claim to a beautifully situated lake, its isolated position towering over the moors of the lonely Migneint makes it a superb vantage point from which to survey all the great mountains of Snowdonia, near and far. Together with its neighbour, Moel Llyfnant, it makes a fine round that few know about.

The walk begins with a mile of tarmac heading eastwards up the road but it is a pleasurable stroll along a quiet lane and makes a gentle leg loosener to start the day. ▶

After this first mile the lane reaches a broad stony track coming down from the right and guarded by metal gates. This is the service road for the reservoir at **Llyn Arenig Fawr**. Turn up this and after an initial climb it levels out and becomes a charming grassy track leading effortlessly into the heart of the mountains with the crags of Y Castell across the waters of the lake.

Those who prefer to get straight down to business can park at the foot of the track to Llyn Arenig but will have to tackle this stretch at the end of a tiring day.

The lake is impounded by a dam and its main purpose is a **reservoir for the Bala area**. A small building below the dam has been converted into a rudimentary refuge by the CLLM, which cares for bothies among the Welsh hills.

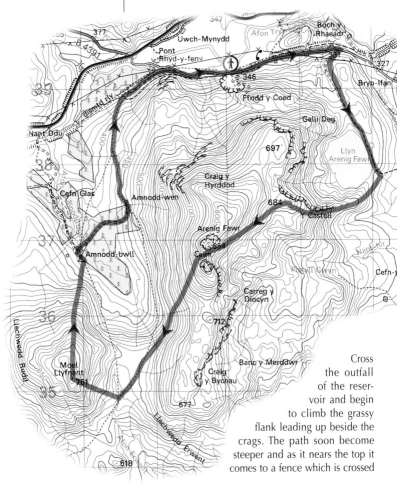

Cross the outfall of the reservoir and begin to climb the grassy flank leading up beside the crags. The path soon become steeper and as it nears the top it comes to a fence which is crossed

Llyn Arenig Fawr

on a makeshift stile of rocks – they are a feature of this walk – before climbing to the top of the slope where the long ridge of **Arenig Fawr** comes into view. Cross a second fence on another rudimentary stile and continue on the grassy path which traverses the long green flank well below the crest. At the end of the traverse it begins a steeper climb through rock and across scree to reach a shoulder where the summit trig point comes into view. Head up to this.

> The 845m (2801ft) **summit of Arenig Fawr** has a windbreak containing a memorial to the crew of a World War II Flying Fortress which crashed into the mountain in 1943, killing all six men on board.
> The summit is a superb viewpoint: its lonely position with no other higher mountains around means there is a 360° panorama of the peaks of the national park and a happy lunch break can be passed trying to identify them.

From the summit continue along the ridge to cross the south summit, then make your way down the ridge. There is no single path and the best guide is the fence to your right, leading down to a flat area of attractive ponds and rocky knolls through which the now clearer path weaves. When it reaches a fence follow it leftwards to another distinctly homemade stile. Cross this and then drop down the slope to the col, making for the clear path visible on the grassy slope of **Moel Llyfnant**. ▶

A path heading northwards from here is a quick escape route if time is pressing or the weather turns nasty.

Traversing the slope to the summit
of Arenig Fawr

This proves to be rocky and attractive with a view almost as good as its slightly higher neighbour.

The track squelches across the col before hurling itself at the slope in a frontal assault. Finally it curls leftwards across the slope before climbing to the 751m (2464ft) summit. ◄

From the summit drop down northwards to the junction of a fence and tumbledown wall and continue on the path heading northwards, making towards the heathery upturned pudding basin of Arenig Fach across the valley. As you descend, sometimes on a grassy path and at others making your own route down steep slopes, the ruined farmhouse of **Amnodd-bwll** comes into view on the edge of the conifer plantations in the valley floor. Aim for this, eventually joining a broad track for the last few metres.

Here the escape route path from the col before Moel Llyfnant joins the route.

At the farmhouse take the forestry track leading away between the buildings and follow it across a bridge as it rises slightly. It reaches the even more dilapidated ruins of a second farmstead, **Amnodd-wen**, where it joins a track coming in from the right. ◄ Pass between the buildings to reach a fork and go left. Where the track appears to end take a fainter, wet path breaking off rightwards to climb back up to a ruined wall and fence. These are followed across waterlogged pastures infested with rushes to a stile beyond which the path steadily improves until it emerges on road used at the start of the walk. Turn right and follow it for about 1km (½ mile) back to the car.

WALK 38

*Cadair Berwyn and
Pistyll Rhaeadr*

Start/Finish	Tan-y-pistyll
Distance	11km (6½ miles)
Total ascent	620m (2030ft)
Grade	Moderate
Time	4hr
Terrain	Good tracks, steep descent
Map	OS Explorer 255 Llangollen and Berwyn
Access	Turn off the B4391 from Bala at Penybontfawr to Llanrhaeadr-ym-Mochnant. Turn left in the village, signed to Pistyll Waterfall and follow the single track road for 6km (3½ miles) to car parks.
Parking	Pay and display car park by the tea shop, free parking in laybys a couple of hundred metres back down the road

The heather-covered Berwyn range somehow escaped inclusion in the national park – with so many mountains to go at it had to stop somewhere – but to a walker's eye it is very definitely worthy of inclusion alongside the other peaks of southern Snowdonia. The sylvan approach is a delight and when you add the dramatic presence of Pistyll Rhaeadr, one of the natural wonders of Wales, the walk becomes a must-do excursion.

On the drive up the valley the top of the falls peep over the trees but it is only when you reach their foot that you appreciate their full majesty and height. The **Afon Disgynfa** plunges 80m (260ft) in two vertical drops separated by a natural rock archway two thirds of the way down. The walk ends by the falls but it is unlikely many visitors will be able to resist looking at them before setting off. And who can blame them? The sight is jaw-dropping.

Having had your fill of the **Pistyll Rhaeadr** falls (and probably sacrificed countless pixels to capturing them) turn back down the road for about 400 metres, ignoring a farm gate on the left, to reach a stile and signed path above the road on the banking on the left. This is the start of a rising grass track which is a pleasure to walk as it heads up the valley, steadily gaining height with fine views of the falls and their flanking woodlands ahead.

As the track turns deeper into the valley the falls are left behind but the pointed south summit of Cadair Berwyn appears ahead. At a fork take the right hand option uphill.

The path crosses stiles and fords a couple of streams as it climbs into the cwm, where at the last moment

Pistyll Rhaeadr

Cadair Berwyn

Llyn Lluncaws is suddenly revealed cupped in the hollow. ▶

From here the path climbs the spur on the left hand side of the cwm before teetering along its rim to a col beneath the final slopes of **Cadair Berwyn**'s south summit.

The top is one of **three summits strung closely together** along the ridge. The south is the highest and fittingly also the most attractive, being marked by a final rocky tor. A second top has a large circular windbreak and the third is home to the trig point, despite being a junior partner in the trio. It was long thought that neighbouring and distinctly less prepossessing Moel Sych was the highest point in the Berwyns, and then it was decided the two mountains were exactly the same height at 827m. More recently, however, this south summit has been elevated to 830m (2722ft), a miniscule but all-important 3m (10ft) higher than both its neighbour and the top marked by the trig point.

This sheet of water, tucked beneath the headwall of the cwm, always appears sombre and dark even on the brightest midsummer days.

Having gained the ridge it would be a simple matter to extend the walk to 700m (2297ft) Cadair Bronwen and back, which would add a total of 5km (3 miles), 210m (685ft) of ascent and a couple of hours to the walk.

From the south summit turn back the way you came but follow the fence line down into the col and up the negligible rise to **Moel-Sych**, whose summit is marked by a sprawling pile of stones on the rounded top. Just before the summit a fence turns leftwards downhill. Follow this down a steep slope. Its arrow-straight line and angle make it a tedious flog as an ascent route but thankfully the soft peat and turf offer a relatively comfortable and direct way down.

As it nears the valley and the woods around the falls the path steepens and meets a broad cross path where it is possible to turn right to a stile and gate leading to the top of the falls. The series of minor cataracts above the falls are attractive and well worth seeing but the main drop is so steep that it is disappointingly invisible from this angle.

WARNING

It should be noted that despite the almost certainly terminal drop from the edge the falls are entirely unfenced so it would be advisable to keep a firm hold of any children or pets in the party.

Here the tea shop provides refreshments.

To reach the valley return to the broad cross path and follow it briefly uphill before heading back down on a zigzag path which leads to the foot of the falls. ◄

THE WELSH 3000S

Looking along the Glyders to Tryfan (Day 1)

THE WELSH 3000S

Looking back across Llyn Bochlwyd to the Glyderau tops (Day 1)

The traverse of the Welsh 3000s is often considered a classic challenge, to be crossed in a single day's run or walk. Fleet-footed runners with leather lungs and iron thighs have completed it in a scarcely credible 4hr 20min, and super-fit walkers will hope to complete the traverse of the 15 peaks in under 12 hours. However, it should be noted that both these times are measured from the summit of the first peak, Snowdon, to the last one, Foel-fras, and gloss over the minor inconveniences of having to climb the highest mountain in England and Wales before you even begin and the long march out at the

northern end of the Carneddau once the clock has stopped.

It all adds up to one of the most demanding challenges in British walking. Even the summit–summit version is around 42km (26 miles) and valley–valley is pushing 50km (31 miles). Both involve around 4000m (13,000ft) of ascent and descent. There are also a few complicated bits of navigation along the way, especially if the attempt ends in the dark.

While completing the round in a day is a feat to be admired many opt to take a little longer, treating the magnificent round as something to be enjoyed rather than endured,

Approaching Drum, the final top (Day 2)

with their eyes on rock rather than the clock. This is best done by treating it as a two or even three-day expedition, which allows the mountains to be savoured while still fitting them into a weekend, and still an energetic and demanding one.

The walk can be undertaken from a base in the Ogwen Valley (youth hostel), travelling round to Pen-y-Pass to begin the walk, spending the middle night at Ogwen before tackling the Carneddau and returning to Ogwen at the end of the day. There is also a splendidly situated youth hostel at Pen-y-Pass itself. Those with the time

to spare for a more leisurely walk could even split the first day still further with an overnight stop at Nant Peris or Llanberis. After all, most walkers would consider the ascent of Crib Goch and Snowdon to be a perfectly respectable day's work in its own right rather than as a mere warm up for a traverse of the Glyderau and Tryfan.

Transport to the start is tricky unless you can organise a support team, and even more so at the end of the walk. Depending on timings, without a chauffeur or a car in position it may be necessary to resort to taxis.

DAY 1
Snowdon and the Glyderau

Start	Pen-y-Pass
Finish	Ogwen
Distance	24km (15 miles)
Total ascent	2420m (7940ft)
Grade	Strenuous/scrambles
Time	10hr
Terrain	Exposed rocky ridge, untracked cwms and high paths
Map	OS OL17 Snowdon/Yr Wyddfa
Access	Pen-y-Pass is at the top of the Llanberis Pass

Facing the towering pyramid of Crib Goch and the knowledge of all the miles and footage that lie beyond it could be a daunting prospect so far better to dwell on the exhilaration that lies ahead over the next few hours instead. This is the finest expedition to be found south of the Roman Wall and the first day is full of adventure, excitement and thrilling landscapes, packing in lots of naked rock and magnificent ridge walking at its very best.

The route starts up the PyG Track, which leaves the top right hand corner of the car park aiming for the shapely cone of Crib Goch, the first objective of the day. Assuming you are setting off early you could well enjoy the rare treat of having the path to yourself. After about ¾hr **Llyn Llydaw** comes into view, with the pointed summit of Snowdon beyond. The main path carries on straight ahead to reach the lake, but a narrower, signed track breaks off rightwards towards **Crib Goch**, the first of the 15 peaks to be climbed.

The route soon becomes a scramble up short walls and polished slabs to the ridge. The crossing ends with three towers, which appear daunting but prove quite straightforward. Beyond the path rises in a series of scrambles over **Crib y Ddysgl** to the trig point on **Garnedd Ugain**, the second top. Carry on to a col

to join the broad path and railway that have come up from Llanberis. Turn left up the ridge to the summit of **Snowdon**.

Crib Goch, the first objective of the day

A glance northwards from here shows there is still a long way to go but you have the **first three peaks under your belt** – including, crucially, the highest

map continues on page 203

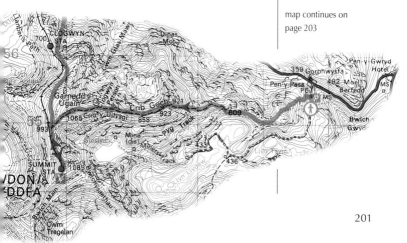

Llanberis Path beside Snowdon Railway

one. Depending on fitness and the size of the rucksack this will take about 2½–3hr.

From here reverse your steps to the col where the PyG Track heads downhill and instead carry on ahead down the path towards Llanberis.

Where the path passes under the railway ignore the tunnel and instead carry on straight ahead down the right hand side of the railway line towards **Clogwyn Station** on a narrow path marked by a single post. The path traverses across the top of one gully, until about halfway to the station buildings it begins to descend a second gully. Initially the path is steep and rough, dropping in a series of zigzags. It descends scree and shale, which can be greasy and tricky in wet conditions, before emerging in the grassy upper cwm where the path becomes fainter and harder to follow but usually runs slightly away from the true left bank of the stream. Do not follow the stream too slavishly, especially in the middle section where it's necessary to take a green ramp leading leftwards as staying too close to the stream will lead you into a band of crags. The track eventually emerges onto the main road down the pass near the houses of **Gwastadnant**. Here turn left down the pass to Nant Peris and the sobering realisation that you are now some 250m (820ft) lower than when you started and facing the 730m (2390ft) ascent of the opposite wall of the pass. ▶

Pass the Vaynol Arms to take a lane on the right by the old chapel and signed to the campsite. Follow the lane as it swings left past the site entrance and some modern houses with vast piles of slate debris filling the view ahead. Where the lane forks by a whitewashed climbing hut go left and after 150 metres or so take the signposted path climbing steeply up the hillside aiming for the hanging valley of the **Afon Dudodyn** below Elidir Fawr's knobbly ridge.

The path carries on beside the stream before reaching a flatter section where the route leaves it to cross a footbridge on the left and begin the climb up the grassy spur towards the crest. After a final boulder field the path delivers you onto the summit of **Elidir Fawr**, with its circular windbreak. The ridge proves to be sharp and the ground drops away steeply on the other side down to the Marchlyn Bach and the curving dam of **Marchlyn Mawr reservoir**, which feeds the power station buried in the 'electric mountain' beneath your feet.

The path follows the ridge eastwards through the boulders and onto wider grassy slopes before narrowing again to a rocky arête which is descended to Bwlch y Marchlyn below the grassy top of **Mynydd Perfedd**.

The next section offers a little respite as the next couple of summits fail to reach the

If you are splitting the walk into three days this will mark the end of the first day.

map continues on page 205

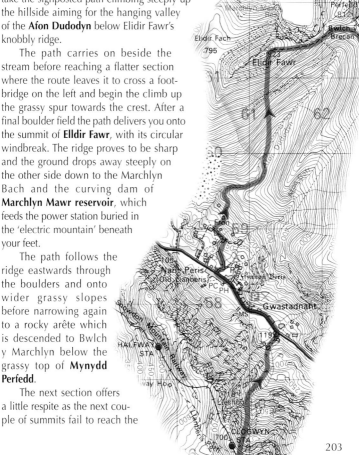

Castell y Gwynt wreathed in mist

There are various paths to the summit and these not always easy to follow in mist thanks to the rocky ground.

magic 3000ft mark and the path bypasses them, aiming for the sharp top of **Y Garn**. From here press on down the ridge, crossing above the exit from the Devil's Kitchen to pass to the left of **Llyn y Cwn** and take the track that begins to climb the rocky slope of **Glyder Fawr**. ◀

From the summit carry on eastwards, aiming for the blocky pyramid of Glyder Fach, a mile away and only a paltry 5m (16ft) lower. The path is rocky but marked by the scuffing of countless boots and the occasional cairn.

As the plateau's boulder field is left behind the path becomes easier to follow and as you drop into the dip between the two Glyders the landmark of the Castell y Gwynt begins to emerge as a collection of pinnacles and huge shards of rock, but exploration must be left for another day. Press on, passing to its right and then climbing up to the jumbled summit rocks of **Glyder Fach** just beyond.

With seven summits behind you all that is left is the day's last one, Tryfan, but this is not to be underestimated, especially at the end of a long day. There are two possible descents, the more direct down the steep, worn scree slope beside Bristly Ridge and the other down the roughly kilometre longer but easier diversion via the Miners' Track.

For both, from the summit carry on in much the same easterly line along the rim of the northern slopes to where a large cairn and the distinctive rocky diving board of the

Cantilever Stone mark the top of Bristly Ridge. Be careful not to be lured down onto the ridge itself, which is tricky in descent. The scree chute to its right is a quick if not particularly pleasant descent to Bwlch Tryfan. Alternatively, scramble through a wide gap in the rocks to the east which reveals the path heading away down the slope towards the distant pool of **Llyn Caseg-fraith**. Drop down towards the llyn but before reaching it a cairn marks the point where the Miners' Track drops down to the left to Bwlch Tryfan.

From here climb the south ridge of **Tryfan** to the summit, which is crowned by the twin pinnacles of Adam and Eve. Record breakers head off towards the North Ridge, turning off to the left before the north summit. However, an easier way down to Ogwen is to reverse the route back to Bwlch Tryfan and then turn right down Cwm Bochlwyd to the overnight stop in Ogwen (reversing the start of Walk 10).

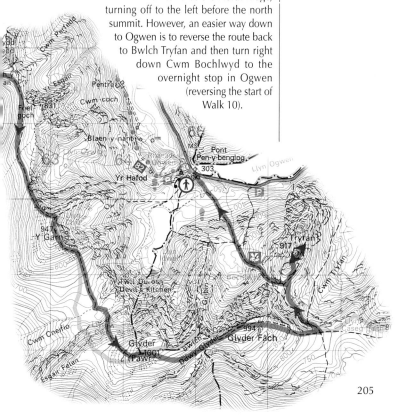

DAY 2
Carneddau

Start	Ogwen
Finish	Pont Newydd
Distance	26km (16 miles)
Total ascent	1560m (5120ft)
Grade	Strenuous
Time	11hr
Terrain	High broad ridges; simple scrambling
Map	OS OL17 Snowdon/Yr Wyddfa
Access	Ogwen is on the A5

Day 2 is in marked contrast to yesterday's route which was over predominantly high rocky ridges and scrambles. The crossing of the Carneddau is a more placid affair, but still involves plenty of climbing and high ridges exposed to the weather, but often over softer ground.

Pen yr Ole Wen, the day's first objective seen across the Ogwen Valley

The day starts with a decision. The first summit is Pen yr Ole Wen and there are two very different ways to tackle it. Speed merchants and the super fit can hurl themselves at the ridge the mountain throws down to Ogwen. Those

feeling the strain of yesterday or looking for a gentler start turn up the pass and take the first lane on the left beyond the lake towards **Tal y Llyn** Farm, passing the MAM climbing hut at Glan Dena. Just before reaching the farm gate take a pitched path heading up the hillside. This climbs beside the stream until it reaches the rim of Cwm Lloer. From here it turns leftwards up the fine ridge, which provides a simple scramble. From the top of the scramble the path continues around the rim of the cwm to **Pen yr Ole Wen**'s bare summit. ▶

Once this has been reached the hardest work has been done and what remains is top quality ridge walking where it is possible to stride out the miles.

The track curves around the cwm, crossing the minor top of **Carnedd Fach** and traversing a wilderness of stones to reach the top of **Carnedd Dafydd**, crowned with a sprawling cairn and windbreaks. From here the broad track carries on around the ridge towards Carnedd Llewelyn.

The path stretches away along the largely featureless ridge before taking a distinct dogleg to the north to begin the climb of the final slopes of

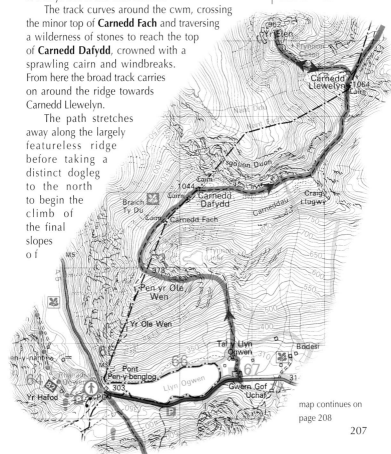

map continues on page 208

207

Carnedd Llewelyn, a great shivering pile of stones. The path arrives at the summit windbreak perched on the eastern rim of the plateau. From here the next summit, Yr Elen, is out of sight and it is necessary to cross to the western rim where the linking path becomes apparent.

This is **a stern test of resolve**, representing a diversion from the main ridge. Yr Elen's summit will demand 90min or more, 190m (620ft) of ascent and 3km (2 miles) of effort just to get back to where you are now. But you've come too far to miss it out now.

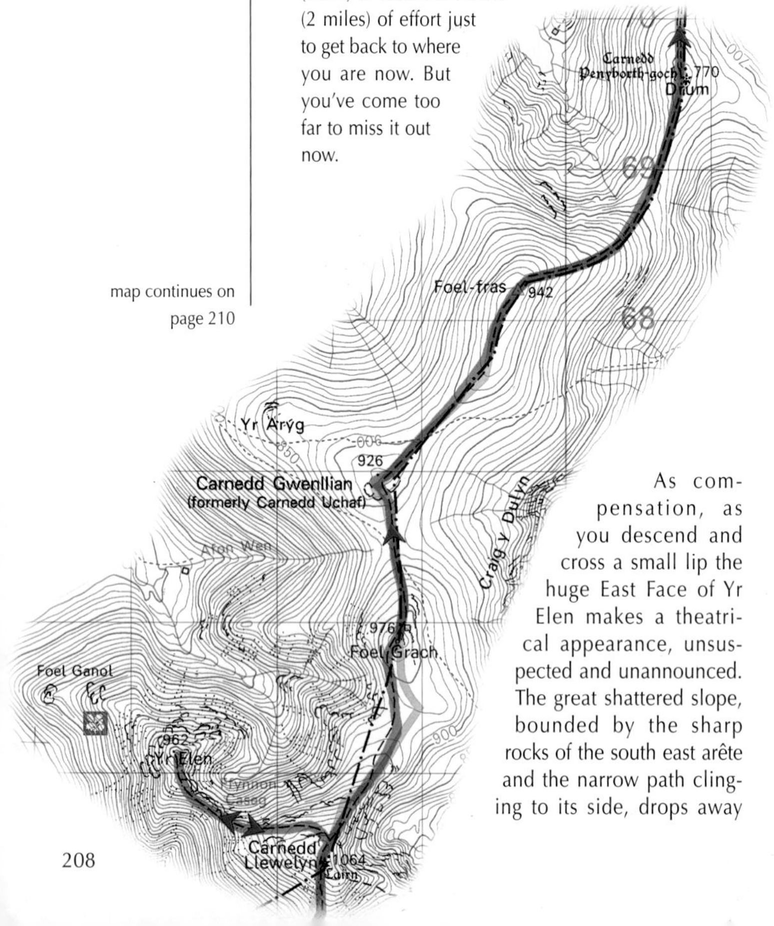

map continues on page 210

Carnedd Penyborth-goch 770
Drum

Foel-fras 942

Yr Arýg 926

Carnedd Gwenllian
(formerly Carnedd Uchaf)

Afon Wen

Craig y Dulyn

976
Foel Grach

Foel Ganol

962
Yr Elen

Ffynnon Caseg

Carnedd Llewelyn 1064
Cairn

As compensation, as you descend and cross a small lip the huge East Face of Yr Elen makes a theatrical appearance, unsuspected and unannounced. The great shattered slope, bounded by the sharp rocks of the south east arête and the narrow path clinging to its side, drops away

hundreds of metres. The summit of **Yr Elen** is a fine iso-lated top from which to survey the central ridge of the Carneddau – including the slope you have just descended and must now reclimb.

The isolated top of Yr Elen

Once back on the main ridge success is more or less assured, even if it is still some way off. Carry on north-wards along the ridge and cross the grassy top of Foel Grach, which has an emergency refuge if needed on the other side.

Next comes the penultimate and most controversial 3000, Carnedd Uchaf which has comparatively recently been given a second name, **Carnedd Gwenllian**.

Carnedd Gwenllian is frequently not included in lists of the Welsh 3000s due to its limited promi-nence above its parent peak, Foel Fras.

The new name commemorates the daughter of Llewelyn, the last Prince of Wales. Her mother, who is commemorated in the name of Yr Elen, died in childbirth and shortly afterwards her father was killed in battle. King Edward I of England saw his chance to disinherit her and imprisoned her in convents for

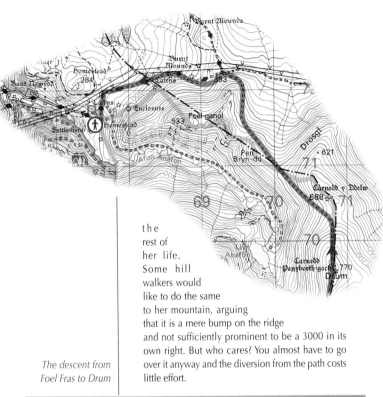

the
rest of
her life.
Some hill
walkers would
like to do the same
to her mountain, arguing
that it is a mere bump on the ridge
and not sufficiently prominent to be a 3000 in its
own right. But who cares? You almost have to go
over it anyway and the diversion from the path costs
little effort.

*The descent from
Foel Fras to Drum*

The final top Foel-fras is in sight. But do not drop your guard. The summit may be the official end of the 3000s walk but you are still at 942m (3089ft) and a long way from home. The shortest route descends the slope northwards to **Llyn Anafon**, but it is steep on tired legs to reach the track to the car park at Pont Newydd, where with luck or good planning a vehicle will be waiting. ▶

The longer but easier variation takes the long grassy descent and climb northwards to **Drum** before continuing down the ridge to join a broad track which weaves its way down to Pont Newydd.

If not take the lane to Abergwyngregyn on the main A55 coast road.

APPENDIX A
Route summary table

Walk	Name	Distance	Ascent/Descent	Grade	Time	Page
1	Tal y Fan	16km (10 miles)	510m (1540ft)	Moderate	4–5hr	24
2	Aber Falls and N Carneddau	20km (12½ miles)	1020m (3350ft)	Strenuous	7hr	28
3	Cwm Eigiau Horseshoe	16km (10 miles)	1075m (3525ft)	Strenuous	6–7hr	33
4	Southern Carneddau	16km (10 miles)	1170m (3840ft)	Strenuous	6hr	38
5	Cwm Llafar Horseshoe	16km (10 miles)	1020m (3350ft)	Strenuous	5–6hr	43
6	Gallt yr Ogof and Y Foel Goch	14km (9 miles)	670m (2198ft)	Moderate	5hr	48
7	Glyderau from Pen-y-Gwryd	10km (6 miles)	804m (2613ft)	Moderate	4–5hr	53
8	Tryfan by North Ridge and Heather Terrace	6km (4 miles)	614m (2014ft)	Strenuous (Scramble)	3–4hr	57
9	Tryfan Without Fears	6.5km (4 miles)	614m (2014ft)	Moderate	3–4hr	61
10	Cwm Bochlwyd and Glyder Fach	8km (5 miles)	850m (2790ft)	Strenuous	5hr	65
11	Y Garn and the Devil's Kitchen	6.5km (4 miles)	641m (2128ft)	Strenuous	4hr	69
12	Elidir Fawr and Y Garn	14km (8½ miles)	1260ft (4134ft)	Strenuous	5hr	73
13	Llyn Crafnant and Llyn Geirionydd	8km (5 miles)	300m (984ft)	Easy	3hr	78
14	Llyn y Parc and Conwy View	10km (6 miles)	500m (1650ft)	Moderate	3hr	81
15	Moel Eilio Horseshoe	14km (9 miles)	990m (3250ft)	Moderate	4–5hr	86

Walk	Name	Distance	Ascent/Descent	Grade	Time	Page
16	Snowdon Horseshoe	11km (7 miles)	1100m (3575ft)	Strenuous (Scramble)	6–7hr	90
17	Snowdon via Miners' and PyG Tracks	11km (7 miles)	750m (2461ft)	Moderate	5–6hr	95
18	Lliwedd via Miners' Track and Y Gribin	11km (7 miles)	539m (1768ft)	Strenuous (Scramble)	4–5hr	99
19	Snowdon via Watkin and Rhyd Ddu Paths	12.5km (8 miles)	1050ft (3445ft)	Strenuous	6hr	103
20	Yr Aran	10km (6 miles)	805m (2640ft)	Moderate	4hr	107
21	Cwm Pennant and the Moel Hebog ridge	15km (9½ miles)	750m (2460ft)	Strenuous	6hr	112
22	Mynydd Mawr	10k (6 miles)	550m (1800ft)	Moderate	3–4hr	117
23	Nantlle Ridge	13k (8 miles)	1025m (3363ft)	Moderate	5–6hr	121
24	Moel Siabod	11km (7 miles)	730m (2395ft)	Moderate	4hr	128
25	Aberglaslyn Gorge and Llyn Dinas	8km (5 miles)	550m (1800ft)	Moderate	3–4hr	132
26	Cnicht and Cwm Croesor	12km (7 miles)	650m (2132ft)	Moderate	4–5hr	137
27	The Moelwyns	10km (6 miles)	780m (2559ft)	Moderate	4–5hr	142
28	Rhinog Fawr by the Roman Steps	8km (5 miles)	610m (2000ft)	Moderate	4–5hr	148
29	Rhinog Fach and Y Llethr	13km (8 miles)	740m (2428m)	Strenuous	5–6hr	152
30	Precipice Walk, Dolgellau	5km (3 miles)	70m (230ft)	Easy	2hr	158
31	Cadair Idris by Pony Path	10km (6 miles)	734m (2420ft)	Moderate	4hr	161
32	Cadair Idris from Minffordd	10km (6 miles)	975m (3200ft)	Strenuous	5–6hr	165

Walk	Name	Distance	Ascent/Descent	Grade	Time	Page
33	Dolgoch Falls and Tarrenhendre	10km (6 miles)	600m (1968ft)	Moderate	4hr	171
34	Rhobell Fawr	13km (8 miles)	575m (1900ft)	Moderate	5hr	176
35	Cwm Cywarch Horseshoe and Aran Fawddwy	12.5km (8 miles)	900m (2950ft)	Moderate	4–5hr	180
36	Traverse of Aran Ridge	15km (9½ miles)	1000m (3281ft)	Moderate	5–6hr	184
37	Arenig Fawr and Moel Llyfnant	16km (10 miles)	850m (2780ft)	Moderate	5–6hr	189
38	Cadair Berwyn and Pistyll Rhaeadr	11km (6½ miles)	620m (2030ft)	Moderate	4hr	193
The Welsh 3000s						
Day 1	Snowdon and the Glyderau	24km (15 miles)	2420m (7940ft)	Strenuous (Scramble)	10hr	200
Day 2	Carneddau	26km (16 miles)	1560m (5120ft)	Strenuous	11hr	206

APPENDIX B

Welsh/English glossary

Contrary to what some paranoid visitors may have you believe, Welsh is not spoken just to exclude the English. It is the everyday language of many in Snowdonia. You will hear it being used widely in pubs, shops and in the street, spoken by everyone from school children to pensioners. Fortunately people also speak English so there is no problem in being understood. Important signs are usually bi-lingual. However, knowing a few words of Welsh does come in useful from time to time, not least in relating the landscape to the map and in knowing what you can and can't do.

These a few of the more useful ones:

aber	river mouth/ estuary/confluence	*drws*	door/pass
		dyffryn	valley
afon	river	*eglwys*	church
allt	hillside/cliff	*fawr*	big
bach (fach)	small	*felin*	mill
bont	bridge	*ffordd*	road
bryn	hill	*ffridd*	high pasture
bwlch	pass/col	*ffynnon*	well/spring
cadair	chair	*foel*	rounded/bare hill
cae	field/enclosure	*glas*	blue/green
caer	fort	*glyder*	heap
capel	chapel	*glyn*	valley
carn/carnedd	cairn	*goch*	red
castell	castle	*gors*	bog
cau	hollow	*gribbin*	ridge
clogwyn	cliff	*hafod*	summer dwelling
coch	red	*hen*	old
coed	wood	*hendre*	winter dwelling
craig	crag	*isaf*	lower
crib	ridge	*llan*	church
cwm	hanging valley/ corrie	*llwybr*	path
		llyn	lake
ddu/du	black	*maen*	stone
dim	no (as in no parking/ camping etc)	*mawr*	big
		melin	mill
dinas	fort/palace	*moel*	rounded hill
drum	ridge	*mynydd*	mountain

nant	stream	*rhyd*	ford
pant	small hollow	*tal*	end
pen	head/top	*twll*	hole
penrhyn	promontory	*ty*	house
plas	large house	*uchaf*	upper
pont	bridge	*wen/wyn*	white
ogof	cave	*y/yr*	the
pwll	pool	*ynys*	island
rhaeadr	waterfall	*ysbyty*	hospital
rhiw	slope	*ysgol*	school
rhos	moor		

APPENDIX C
Useful contacts

Accommodation
www.visitsnowdonia.info

www.snowdoniatourism.co.uk

www.yha.org.uk

Mountain rescue (all teams)
Dial 999 and ask for the Police and
then Mountain Rescue

National Park information
www.eryri-npa.gov.uk

Information offices
Betws-y-Coed
tel 01690 710426

Beddgelert
tel 01766 890615

Dolgellau
tel 01341 422888

Aberdyfi
tel 01654 767321

Public transport
Conwy Council publish a combined
bus timetable
tel 01492 575412
www.conwy.gov.uk

Gwynedd Council public transport
information
tel 01286 679535

Ffestiniog and Welsh Highland Railways
Harbour Station
Porthmadog
Gwynedd
LL49 9NF
tel 01766 516000
www.festrail.co.uk

Talyllyn Railway
Wharf Station
Tywyn
Gwynedd
LL36 9EY
tel 01654 710472
www.talyllyn.co.uk

Weather forecasts
Met Office
www.metoffice.gov.uk

Mountain Weather Information Service
www.mwis.org.uk

NOTES

NOTES

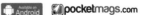

LISTING OF CICERONE GUIDES

SCOTLAND

Backpacker's Britain:
  Northern Scotland
Ben Nevis and Glen Coe
Cycling in the Hebrides
Great Mountain Days in Scotland
Mountain Biking in Southern and
  Central Scotland
Mountain Biking in West and North
  West Scotland
Not the West Highland Way
Scotland
Scotland's Best Small Mountains
Scotland's Mountain Ridges
Scrambles in Lochaber
The Ayrshire and Arran
  Coastal Paths
The Border Country
The Cape Wrath Trail
The Great Glen Way
The Great Glen Way Map Booklet
The Hebridean Way
The Hebrides
The Isle of Mull
The Isle of Skye
The Skye Trail
The Southern Upland Way
The Speyside Way
The Speyside Way Map Booklet
The West Highland Way
Walking Highland Perthshire
Walking in Scotland's Far North
Walking in the Angus Glens
Walking in the Cairngorms
Walking in the Ochils, Campsie
  Fells and Lomond Hills
Walking in the Pentland Hills
Walking in the Southern Uplands
Walking in Torridon
Walking Loch Lomond and
  the Trossachs
Walking on Arran
Walking on Harris and Lewis
Walking on Rum and the
  Small Isles
Walking on the Orkney and
  Shetland Isles
Walking on Uist and Barra
Walking the Corbetts
  Vol 1 South of the Great Glen
Walking the Corbetts
  Vol 2 North of the Great Glen
Walking the Galloway Hills
Walking the Munros
  Vol 1 – Southern, Central and
  Western Highlands

Walking the Munros
  Vol 2 – Northern Highlands and
  the Cairngorms
West Highland Way Map Booklet
Winter Climbs Ben Nevis and
  Glen Coe
Winter Climbs in the Cairngorms

NORTHERN ENGLAND TRAILS

Hadrian's Wall Path
Hadrian's Wall Path Map Booklet
Pennine Way Map Booklet
The Coast to Coast Map Booklet
The Coast to Coast Walk
The Dales Way
The Dales Way Map Booklet
The Pennine Way

LAKE DISTRICT

Cycling in the Lake District
Great Mountain Days in the
  Lake District
Lake District Winter Climbs
Lake District: High Level and
  Fell Walks
Lake District: Low Level and
  Lake Walks
Mountain Biking in the Lake District
Scrambles in the Lake District
  – North
Scrambles in the Lake District
  – South
Short Walks in Lakeland Books 1–3
The Cumbria Way
The Southern Fells
Tour of the Lake District
Trail and Fell Running in the
  Lake District

NORTH WEST ENGLAND
AND THE ISLE OF MAN

Cycling the Pennine Bridleway
Cycling the Way of the Roses
Isle of Man Coastal Path
The Lancashire Cycleway
The Lune Valley and Howgills
The Ribble Way
Walking in Cumbria's Eden Valley
Walking in Lancashire
Walking in the Forest of Bowland
  and Pendle
Walking on the Isle of Man
Walking on the West
  Pennine Moors
Walks in Lancashire Witch Country
Walks in Ribble Country
Walks in Silverdale and Arnside

NORTH EAST ENGLAND,
YORKSHIRE DALES AND
PENNINES

Cycling in the Yorkshire Dales
Great Mountain Days in
  the Pennines
Mountain Biking in the
  Yorkshire Dales
South Pennine Walks
St Oswald's Way and
  St Cuthbert's Way
The Cleveland Way and the
  Yorkshire Wolds Way
The Cleveland Way Map Booklet
The North York Moors
The Reivers Way
The Teesdale Way
Walking in County Durham
Walking in Northumberland
Walking in the North Pennines
Walking in the Yorkshire Dales:
  North and East
Walking in the Yorkshire Dales:
  South and West
Walks in Dales Country
Walks in the Yorkshire Dales

WALES AND WELSH BORDERS

Cycling Lôn Las Cymru
Glyndwr's Way
Great Mountain Days in Snowdonia
Hillwalking in Shropshire
Hillwalking in Wales – Vols 1 & 2
Mountain Walking in Snowdonia
Offa's Dyke Map Booklet
Offa's Dyke Path
Pembrokeshire Coast Path
  Map Booklet
Ridges of Snowdonia
Scrambles in Snowdonia
The Ascent of Snowdon
The Ceredigion and Snowdonia
  Coast Paths
The Pembrokeshire Coast Path
The Severn Way
The Snowdonia Way
The Wales Coast Path
The Wye Valley Walk
Walking in Carmarthenshire
Walking in Pembrokeshire
Walking in the Forest of Dean
Walking in the South Wales Valleys
Walking in the Wye Valley
Walking on the Brecon Beacons
Walking on the Gower
Welsh Winter Climbs

DERBYSHIRE, PEAK DISTRICT AND MIDLANDS

Cycling in the Peak District
Dark Peak Walks
Scrambles in the Dark Peak
Walking in Derbyshire
White Peak Walks:
    The Northern Dales
White Peak Walks:
    The Southern Dales

SOUTHERN ENGLAND

20 Classic Sportive Rides
    in South East England
20 Classic Sportive Rides
    in South West England
Cycling in the Cotswolds
Mountain Biking on the
    North Downs
Mountain Biking on the
    South Downs
North Downs Way Map Booklet
South West Coast Path Map Booklet
    – Vols 1–3
Suffolk Coast and Heath Walks
The Cotswold Way
The Cotswold Way Map Booklet
The Great Stones Way
The Kennet and Avon Canal
The Lea Valley Walk
The North Downs Way
The Peddars Way and Norfolk
    Coast Path
The Pilgrims' Way
The Ridgeway Map Booklet
The Ridgeway National Trail
The South Downs Way
The South Downs Way
    Map Booklet
The South West Coast Path
The Thames Path
The Thames Path Map Booklet
The Two Moors Way
Walking Hampshire's Test Way
Walking in Cornwall
Walking in Essex
Walking in Kent
Walking in London
Walking in Norfolk
Walking in Sussex
Walking in the Chilterns
Walking in the Cotswolds
Walking in the Isles of Scilly
Walking in the New Forest
Walking in the North
    Wessex Downs
Walking in the Thames Valley
Walking on Dartmoor
Walking on Guernsey
Walking on Jersey

Walking on the Isle of Wight
Walking the Jurassic Coast
Walks in the South Downs
    National Park

BRITISH ISLES CHALLENGES, COLLECTIONS AND ACTIVITIES

The Book of the Bivvy
The Book of the Bothy
The C2C Cycle Route
The End to End Cycle Route
The Mountains of England and
    Wales: Vol 1 Wales
The Mountains of England and
    Wales: Vol 2 England
The National Trails
The UK's County Tops
Three Peaks, Ten Tors

ALPS CROSS-BORDER ROUTES

100 Hut Walks in the Alps
Across the Eastern Alps: E5
Alpine Ski Mountaineering Vol 1 –
    Western Alps
Alpine Ski Mountaineering Vol 2 –
    Central and Eastern Alps
Chamonix to Zermatt
The Karnischer Hohenweg
The Tour of the Bernina
Tour of Mont Blanc
Tour of Monte Rosa
Tour of the Matterhorn
Trail Running – Chamonix and the
    Mont Blanc region
Trekking in the Alps
Trekking in the Silvretta and
    Rätikon Alps
Trekking Munich to Venice
Walking in the Alps

PYRENEES AND FRANCE/SPAIN CROSS-BORDER ROUTES

The GR10 Trail
The GR11 Trail
The Pyrenean Haute Route
The Pyrenees
The Way of St James – Spain
Walks and Climbs in the Pyrenees

AUSTRIA

Innsbruck Mountain Adventures
The Adlerweg
Trekking in Austria's Hohe Tauern
Trekking in the Stubai Alps
Trekking in the Zillertal Alps
Walking in Austria

SWITZERLAND

Cycle Touring in Switzerland
The Swiss Alpine Pass Route –
    Via Alpina Route 1

The Swiss Alps
Tour of the Jungfrau Region
Walking in the Bernese Oberland
Walking in the Valais
Walks in the Engadine –
    Switzerland

FRANCE

Chamonix Mountain Adventures
Cycle Touring in France
Cycling London to Paris
Cycling the Canal du Midi
Écrins National Park
Mont Blanc Walks
Mountain Adventures in the
    Maurienne
The GR20 Corsica
The GR5 Trail
The GR5 Trail – Vosges and Jura
The Grand Traverse of the
    Massif Central
The Loire Cycle Route
The Moselle Cycle Route
The River Rhone Cycle Route
The Robert Louis Stevenson Trail
The Way of St James – Le Puy to
    the Pyrenees
Tour of the Oisans: The GR54
Tour of the Queyras
Vanoise Ski Touring
Via Ferratas of the French Alps
Walking in Corsica
Walking in Provence – East
Walking in Provence – West
Walking in the Auvergne
Walking in the Briançonnais
Walking in the Cevennes
Walking in the Dordogne
Walking in the Haute Savoie: North
Walking in the Haute Savoie: South
Walks in the Cathar Region

GERMANY

Hiking and Biking in the
    Black Forest
The Danube Cycleway Volume 1
The Rhine Cycle Route
The Westweg
Walking in the Bavarian Alps

ICELAND AND GREENLAND

Walking and Trekking in Iceland

IRELAND

The Irish Coast to Coast Walk
The Mountains of Ireland
The Wild Atlantic Way and
    Western Ireland

For full information on all our
guides, books and eBooks,
visit our website:
www.cicerone.co.uk

Walking – Trekking – Mountaineering – Climbing – Cycling

Over 40 years, Cicerone have built up an outstanding collection of over 300 guides, inspiring all sorts of amazing adventures.

 Every guide comes from extensive exploration and research by our expert authors, all with a passion for their subjects. They are frequently praised, endorsed and used by clubs, instructors and outdoor organisations.

All our titles can now be bought as **e-books**, **ePubs** and **Kindle** files and we also have an online magazine – **Cicerone Extra** – with features to help cyclists, climbers, walkers and trekkers choose their next adventure, at home or abroad.

Our website shows any **new information** we've had in since a book was published. Please do let us know if you find anything has changed, so that we can publish the latest details. On our **website** you'll also find great ideas and lots of detailed information about what's inside every guide and you can buy **individual routes** from many of them online.

It's easy to keep in touch with what's going on at Cicerone by getting our monthly **free e-newsletter**, which is full of offers, competitions, up-to-date information and topical articles. You can subscribe on our home page and also follow us on **Facebook** and **Twitter** or dip into our **blog**.

Cicerone – the very best guides for exploring the world.

CICERONE

Juniper House, Murley Moss, Oxenholme Road, Kendal, Cumbria LA9 7RL
Tel: 015395 62069 info@cicerone.co.uk
www.cicerone.co.uk